...s of standing water
will have to consider
In a survival situation
that far familiar wild
whenever possible

...able to go for days
...uld supply Even in the
...n maintaining healthy
...ctivities diet is essential
...nd peace of mind. Native
...that will let you survive
...eat the wrong plant.

...n as much as possible
...lva of the region where you
... can provide you with
...situation. Plants can
...s and raw materials
...uld ones. Plants can
... for poisons
...camouflaging

wild food

For Rachel Clare Mears

18 November 1955 – 16 May 2006

RAY MEARS

AND GORDON HILLMAN

wild food

HODDER &
STOUGHTON

Also by Ray Mears

BUSHCRAFT

ESSENTIAL BUSHCRAFT

THE REAL HEROES OF TELEMARK

BUSHCRAFT SURVIVAL

CONTENTS

Introduction

Introduction

The very fabric and scale of a modern city convey a sense of timeless permanence; our modern way of life seems to have existed for ever. Our ancestors, who once hunted and gathered where restaurants and supermarkets stand today, are but a dim and distant memory – indeed, so distant that they would be but a figment of our imagination were it not for the many stone tools they left behind. But that is the effect of the human condition – despite our collective intellect and sophistication we are a myopic species; when it comes to 'time' we struggle to maintain any sense of history beyond the span of a few generations; events that preceded our recorded history are less mysterious than they are unimportant. But if we take the past two thousand years, the span of recorded British history, and compare it with the archaeological history of human presence in Britain, it is but a drop in the ocean.

It was during the Ice Ages that the characteristic human silhouette was first seen against the British skyline. These early ancestors walked upright through a complicated period of geologic history, which saw our climate oscillating from extremely cold 'glacial' periods to warmer 'interglacial' and shorter 'interstadial' periods. Five times, intense cold brought the northern ice sheets southwards far enough for them to extend across most of Britain. Consequently, because of its geographical location, Britain has always been the frontier of human expansion in north-west Europe as people were driven south.

So far archaeologists have been able to find only traces of early human activity in association with warm interglacial periods, suggesting that our early populations were forced to retreat at those times when the temperature dropped. Eight periods of interglacial occupation have been identified, the latest of which we are still experiencing today. To date the earliest evidence for humans in Britain comes from Pakefield in Suffolk and has been dated to 700,000 BC. The find comprises a collection of thirty-two small pieces of flint, all of which show unmistakable evidence of having been worked by people. Although a modest find, these few flints that were once cast aside as insignificant by their makers have helped to throw new light on early human migration in our corner of Palaeolithic Earth. Without any human remains it is uncertain which of our ancestors left these flint tools, though from their date we can assume that they were made by a species related to ourselves that has been named Heidelberg Human, *Homo heidelbergensis*.

Boxgrove

One of the greatest difficulties in the study of early people is the almost total lack of body remains to investigate. When these do occur they are usually fragmentary, making clear definition of species extremely difficult. New partial remains are therefore of immense importance. In 1993, at Boxgrove, near Chichester, West Sussex, a tibia was discovered, along with two incisor teeth – the remains have been dated to 500,000 BC. This is the earliest fossil evidence of humans yet found in Britain. Under the directorship of Mark Roberts, investigations there have unearthed the largest preserved Palaeolithic land surface in Europe, yielding a remarkable picture of the past.

At the time these items were deposited Britain was still attached to the European mainland. Animal remains unearthed at the site reveal quite a different view of the Britain we know today. There were species we are familiar with, such as robins, starlings, tawny owls, eels, trout, grass snakes, red deer, fallow deer and hedgehogs. But there were also lions, elephants, rhinoceros, spotted hyena, bison, cave bears and giant deer. Indeed, the human tibia showed signs of having been gnawed by a carnivore, possibly a wolf.

Hand axe found at Boxgrove – at the time these were in use they were the principle butchery tool.

This shin bone was long and robust, indicating that this early Briton, also believed to be from the species *Homo heidelbergensis*, stood around 1.8 metres tall and had a well-built musculature. We know virtually nothing about these people's lives. Much of what we do know has been learned from Boxgrove. The tool that most characterises these people is a bifacially worked, ovate hand axe, called by archaeologists the Acheulian Axe. These are found across southern Britain and into the Midlands, but not beyond. Beautiful tools, they blend function with an elegant symmetry. I love to replicate these tools, as it enables me to step into the mind of Boxgrove Man. Working the tool with hard stone hammers, it is possible to feel, smell (for breaking flint has its own dusty odour) and hear the past. The ovate shape is intriguing; while infinitely practical, its symmetry speaks of something more. The challenge of producing this balanced symmetry comes from deep within our psyche – a pressing need to achieve an aesthetic harmony. For me the Acheulian Axe lies at the very roots of art and design; every great gallery should have one displayed in its entrance, reminding us of our origins and the great unknown artists of prehistory.

What is fascinating about Boxgrove is that it has been possible to learn more about these tools' usage. Within the excavations the remains of a wild horse were unearthed, with associated flint working. From careful, detailed analysis of these finds, both the bone remains and the flint, it has been possible to reconstruct a remarkable vignette of past activity. It seems likely that the horse was brought down by early hunters who used projectiles, perhaps sharpened wooden javelins, one of which caused damage to the horse's shoulder blade. From waste flakes found near by it is clear that several flint hand axes were manufactured to butcher it. The horse was then skinned and cut up. Butchery marks left by the hand axes on the bones have proved to be very revealing. I have witnessed similar processes among many hunter-gatherer groups but this site particularly reminds me of meals I have shared with the Hadza in Tanzania, the only difference being that some or all (depending upon the size of the kill) of the animal is cooked on-site. No evidence for fire has yet been found at Boxgrove. Once it is cooked, the Hadza eat the meat by holding the joint between the teeth and slicing off a portion with a knife. The human incisors found at Boxgrove show cut marks, which may be consistent with this technique. Interestingly, the Hadza also break open the bones to consume the marrow, evidence of which has also been found at Boxgrove.

Swanscombe

One of the great mysteries of this early human history is the question of when we first started to use fire. In British archaeology use of fire is not evident until 400,000 BC at the Beeches Pit site in Suffolk. Here, beside the shores of an ancient lake, the remains of campfires have been unearthed; beside these fires flint tools were being made and fragments of bone survive within the hearths themselves.

No human remains have been found at Beeches Pit, but at more or less the same time people were foraging along the south bank of the River Thames. At Swanscombe, close to the river crossing at present-day Dartford, three skull fragments were found, the remains of a woman who shared some features with another early human species, Neanderthal Human, *Homo neanderthalensis*. Often referred to as proto-Neanderthals, individuals such as the Swanscombe lady seem to represent the evolution of *H. neanderthalensis* from *H. heidelbergensis*.

Fully Neanderthal people appear in the archaeological record around 130,000 BC. They are our close cousins yet they have suffered in historic literature. We are left with the impression of a rather less than intelligent, brutish forebear. In fact recent evidence has totally disproved this view. Neanderthals were shorter than us and powerfully built, a body-shape characteristic that is well suited to a cold climate. Capable, brave hunters, they worked flint with a more advanced technique and employed a more sophisticated toolkit than their precursors. Neanderthal finds from other parts of Europe and the Middle East demonstrate the earliest evidence for a spiritual nature. They buried their dead in the foetal position, and sprinkled them with red ochre and wild flowers. Their presence in Britain cannot be considered in any way insignificant, lasting until somewhere in the region of 35,000 BC. Some of the most exciting recent finds are Neanderthal. At Lynford Quarry in Norfolk over two thousand bones, tusks and teeth of mammoth have been found, along with remains from woolly rhinoceros, bison, wolf and brown bear. Hundreds of stone tools were also found, many still fresh and sharp despite being over 60,000 years old. Again, the site preserves hard evidence of butchering, including reindeer and horse bones, which show the characteristic signs of having been broken open for the marrow. I hope that in time more information will be recovered from this fascinating period in our history.

Hadza cooking a small antelope that has just been killed; they even eat the bone marrow. For most of history this would have been a common sight, and we still carry the instincts for this in our psyche.

Homo sapiens

Another great mystery is what happened to the Neanderthals, for perhaps within Britain, and certainly within Europe, Neanderthals would have lived alongside our direct ancestors, the so-called Wise Humans, *Homo sapiens*. In Kent's Cavern, Torquay, the partial remains of a human jawbone have been found. Marks on the bone suggest that this individual was eaten by a hyena, but it is not known whether the jaw was from a Neanderthal or a fully modern human. It is hoped that new testing may provide the answer. Recently dated to between 37,000 and 40,000 BC, the jaw will prove either a very early date for *Homo sapiens* presence in Britain or a late presence for *Homo neanderthalensis*.

Currently the best-confirmed date for the presence of our direct ancestors in Britain is provided by Goat's Hole Cave, Paviland, Wales, dated to 27,000 BC. Here the remains of a young man aged between twenty-five and thirty, about 1.74 metres tall and weighing 11 stone (73 kilos), were found. Headless, the body had been buried in the cave with mammoth ivory rods, a bracelet and animal remains, and had been covered with red ochre and periwinkle shells. But perhaps most importantly, DNA analysis of the body suggests that today's European population evolved from these hunter-gatherers rather than the early farmers who arrived much later in the so-called Neolithic period, at around 4000 BC. This is a very significant finding that not only links us directly to our hunter-gatherer ancestors but also sheds light on the health implications of our modern diet and lifestyle.

The scratch marks on this bone are clear evidence of our early ancestors' butchery techniques.

Bushman in the Kalahari. Traps like this would have been used in Britain to catch small game and they are still of great importance to hunter-gatherers. The older generation who live this life most fully are gradually disappearing and with them, their expertise.

Hunting and gathering

The ravages of time are hard on the remains of the past; despite the evidence of hunting from recovered bone deposits, we actually know very little about our ancestors' diets. Virtually nothing survives in the way of plant remains, and where they have, poor archaeological recovery has usually failed to search for, let alone recover, such information. Today more thorough archaeological techniques are beginning to salvage tantalising organic clues about the plant content of our past meals.

One thing we can be certain about: from the tools, butchery remains and omnivorous dentition left behind by all our early ancestors, we know that they shared a similar way of life – they were all hunter-gatherers. In fact, worldwide, hunting and gathering have been the main means by which our species and those immediately preceding us have made our living, a way of life that began to disappear around thirteen thousand years ago with early attempts at cultivation. Eventually farming, a new experiment in food provision, emerged in several different parts of the world independently, and rapidly spread around the globe, reaching British shores around six thousand years ago. Although hunting remained of importance to early farmers, the pure hunter-gatherer way of life was replaced, a process that is still continuing as I write these lines today. Remote hunter-gatherer groups such as the San bushmen in southern Africa are being encouraged to become herdsmen; the Hadza of Tanzania have to deal with grazing pressure from nomadic pastoralists and migrant cattle farmers; while in South America forest tribes are having to adapt to the loss of their rainforest as the timber is logged out and the ground planted with soya or converted to cattle production. Apart from the North Andaman islanders, who have shut out the modern world, every hunter-gatherer community is facing what seems to be inevitable change. Almost certainly, within the next generation hunting and gathering will cease to exist on Earth. While some would argue that this is an inevitable consequence of our ever-evolving human society, there is also a considerable loss of very specific and beneficial knowledge. Although this is a generalisation, hunter-gatherer societies are based more on adapting society to nature than arrogantly transforming nature to suit human needs. In the light of the ever-increasing weight of evidence that now indicates the damage and pollution we have caused to our environment in the past thousand years, we may yet need to reinvestigate the traditions, wisdom and knowledge of the less damaging lifestyles of hunter-gatherers. Old wisdom may yet combine with new technologies to find a healthy and sustainable way forward for humanity.

Investigating the Mesolithic

This project did not arise out of a search for tribal wisdom that may point the way forward, however, although it has caused us to reflect deeply on the way in which our landscape and habitat have been affected by human activity over the last six thousand years. Rather it arose from a chance introduction to my fellow author Gordon Hillman. A professor of archaeo-botany, Gordon is widely acknowledged to be a world authority on the origins of the early hunter-gatherer diet of the Near East and the beginnings of cultivation, largely through his extensive work at Abu Hurerya in Syria, where it has been possible to study a community as it changed from hunting and gathering to early cultivation. But more than this he is a naturalist of the old school with an active and enquiring curiosity about all things natural. At our first meeting we discussed wild foods and found common interests. I asked him whether he knew what our hunter-gatherers had eaten as staple foods. His answer was both surprising and inspirational: 'Well, we don't really know'. And so began a journey in search of clues, which has so far taken us some ten years to complete and which has led us far and wide, even to the other side of the world. Along the way we have been forced to totally rethink ideas and botanical knowledge that both we and the scientific community have held to be true. We have been able to glimpse and taste the world of our ancestors, but above all we have developed a totally new respect and appreciation for the accomplishments and ability of our hunter-gatherer ancestors.

Faced with some years of British hunting and gathering, during which time our climate and geography have varied widely, we thought it was vital that we should target one particular period for our study. We therefore elected to investigate the Mesolithic period, 8300–4000 BC, particularly the late Mesolithic. This represents the last epoch of British hunting and gathering prior to the arrival of farming, and it is reasonable to assume that it also represents the zenith of British hunter-gatherer technology. Conveniently, it is also a period with many similarities to Britain today.

Britain's Last Hunter-Gatherers

Britains Last Hunter-Gatherers

I've always thought that archaeologists are probably the luckiest scientists of all, because they get nearer to time travel as anyone else I've ever met. In our research into the foods of the past I had great faith that archaeology would be of importance to us – which it was, but it could answer only a very few questions, because our hunter-gatherer ancestors lived so long ago that virtually nothing remains.

Whole hazelnuts

Off the west coast of Skye and to the west of the island of Jura are the two small islands of Oronsay and Colonsay. And there on Colonsay, in a sheltered bay, an amazing discovery was made by Dr Steven Mithen from Reading University. He uncovered an archaeological site that was of tremendous importance to us and our project. He found evidence of a very short period of time, perhaps only a few days in duration, maybe a week at most, when people visited the island to collect and prepare hazelnuts. Today there are very few hazel trees left on the island – most of it is bare. Standing on the shore while we were filming, we could imagine boats arriving in this sheltered bay, where the land

Right: hazelnuts ready for cooking. This may have been a common sight in the British Mesolithic, when hazelnuts are believed to have been a staple of our diet.
Overleaf: this rock shelter near Apple Cross, Scotland, was a temporary home for British hunter-gatherers during the Mesolithic. The slope in front is largely comprised of waste shells and bowls from our ancestors' meals. The same foods can be found today within a stone's throw of the shelter.

was covered in hazel trees, and on the beach, or just above the beach, on a flat, level area, people camping – it was the perfect place to camp – and cooking hazelnuts, some seven and a half thousand years ago. Steven's team uncovered the remains of cooking pits, from which we were able to reconstruct a method of cooking hazelnuts in use in the past. And they found a huge quantity of fragmentary, charred hazelnuts. I've got some of them in my hand, still quite clearly hazelnuts. I find it intriguing that these partially charred remains have survived through all that period of time. In fact, in terms of organic materials, it's only things that are charred which tend to survive. Gordon is a real expert at identifying charred plant remains. He has a library of similar materials that he can use for comparison.

What our ancestors did was to place hazelnuts into shallow depressions in the sand, cover them with sand and then light fires on top. We experimented with this method of cooking to the point where we now feel that we've perfected it. If, at Christmas, say, you sit down to eat a bowlful of hazelnuts, you get to about twelve or maybe twenty if you're lucky, then your mouth dries up and it's difficult to eat any more. But when you cook them, they are totally transformed. All of a sudden a dry resource that's difficult to digest becomes an easily digested potato-like food, and you can sit and eat two hundred without any difficulty at all. Here was our first inkling of the sophistication of our ancestors. A food that we thought we already knew about was being used in a very different way. And this was important to understand, because it meant that apart from looking for evidence of foods we didn't know about, we would also have to take a fresh view of things we already considered to be edible, and think that perhaps there was another way in which these foods were being used.

A shallow pit is created and filled with hazelnuts. Then the pit is sealed and a fire is lit on top and left to burn out – the cooked nuts are now transformed by the heat and are very tasty.

One of the things we discovered by accident, if you like – and we discovered quite a few things by accident during our project was that the hazelnuts, once they've been cooked, preserve really well. I have a bag of hazelnuts that we cooked three years ago which are still edible and tasty now. So it may be that people were cooking some of the hazelnuts for their own consumption, while roasting others for transportation back to a community somewhere else. Of course, the other thing about this site is the fact that you can only get to the island by boat, and no one has yet found evidence of a boat capable of the journey that these people were making at that time. It's tantalising – you can sit there on the shore, and in your mind hear the sound of people coming round the headland, saying, 'There's the place' or 'That's a good place to stop', and making their way onshore. But how they travelled there we'll never know.

The real problem with all this archaeology, of course, is that organic remains from the past survive so poorly. What we do have is lots of evidence of the use of stone tools – countless thousands of projectile points made from flint, and other flint tools. The Mesolithic is an interesting period in that all of a sudden people start to use tiny little tools – microliths – which also raises questions as to why there was a sudden change in the tool typology. If you like, trying to peer into the Mesolithic past through the world of archaeology is rather like trying to read the title on the conductor's score in the Albert Hall by looking through a keyhole in one of the back rooms. It's so difficult to try to piece together our past. Even when we look at Danish Mesolithic sites, where they have more finds preserved by waterlogging, more organic remains, we still have a very narrow window on the past. It's tremendously important to understand that our ancestors weren't just using plants for food – food would have had a much more significant role in their everyday lives than the archaeology can show us today.

We collated what information we could find on organic remains, both from Britain and, widening our net, other parts of Europe, especially Denmark, where, for example, the yellow waterlily seed has been found preserved in sites. Only the tiniest remains survive. These are literally, as I've said before, morsels that have fallen into the ashes at the bottom of the fire and have not been properly consumed, just charred. That's all that remains for us to explore in terms of organic materials, although at other sites we do find preservation in rubbish heaps. In another area of Scotland, at Applecross, we visited a rock shelter, and there in front of the rock shelter were midden mounds. These are the rubbish heaps from 9000 BC. And in these heaps all sorts of things were found: razor shells, limpets and limpet shells, cockles, winkles, seal bones, wild boar remains, bird remains and bones, and also the remains of fish, some of which were deep-water species such as cod, which suggests that our ancestors used nets capable of fishing beyond the shore. Again, these are tantalising clues to a long-vanished culture.

Food for free

So archaeology would play only a small role, it seemed, in guiding us into the past, but one that encouraged us to retain an open mind as to the larger implications of the use of wild foods. The next thing we had to explore was the existing literature. What do we know about the edible foods of Britain today? There are a number of popular titles that have been written over the years, the most famous of which is *Food for Free* by Richard Mabey, a very popular book which has served for several decades now to guide us to the use of wild foods in the countryside. Perhaps the best book available was written by C. Pierpoint Johnson in 1826. I would say his is the most thorough current existing guide to the edible plants of Britain. But even he had to note that by the time he had started to record the information much of the knowledge had already disappeared. In fact, far more knowledge had disappeared from accepted wisdom than we realised, because by the time people in Britain started to keep written records hunter-gatherers had already been extinct for thousands of years. The problem with the existing literature is that, again, it doesn't direct us to foods that could be used as staples. It's very good at providing additions for salads, things that we can do in a country cottage to produce jams and preserves, but it doesn't suggest the basis of a hunter-gatherer's diet, or address in any way the difficulties they would have faced. In truth, the authors never intended to do this.

Above: a Mesolithic mattock head made from red-deer antler. Tools like this were widely used throughout the period for food collecting and were very versatile. We believe they were largely used as digging tools for roots, and there is evidence from Perthshire that they were used to cut up a beached whale. They were very common and are found throughout the western hemisphere.

Left: it's only by reconstructing these tools that we can appreciate their real utility. We found this one very useful for gathering varieties of underground roots.

The botanic jigsaw

So, there again, only part of the story could be gleaned from this information. The next thing to do was to try to piece together what plants were here during the Mesolithic. For this we could use pollen core analysis of samples of soil taken from sedimentary layers deep underground, all the way back to the Mesolithic landscape, to see what pollen remains were to be found. But even this would provide only a partial picture, because not all pollen survives. Most trees are wind-pollinated and produce vast quantities of pollen that are carried far and wide. Some ends up in the peat bogs and lakes, and hence is preserved. However, trees such as pine and field maple are insect-pollinated, as are most herbaceous plants. Their pollen drops straight to the ground and rarely gets carried to peat bogs or lakes – so hardly ever survives. So we had to look at the habitats that existed and assume that certain plants are likely to have been here too. These are the missing pieces in the jigsaw puzzle of which we have the basic framework. Some of these plants we knew were likely to be edible, because of existing knowledge, but others we could not be certain of, and in these cases we would have to look at other parts of the world. Were our plants being used by other indigenous groups around the world for which there might be anthropological evidence, ethnographic records that could guide us? And if not the exact same plant, were there similar related plants, genetic cousins to our plants, having similar properties, that were being used in other parts of the world? It was exactly this sort of information which led us to look at a relative of the sea-kale, the roots of which are still used in Turkmenistan. And that led us to investigate sea-kale here, almost certainly an incredibly important staple food during the Mesolithic period.

Of course, we can't be sure that the things we have found to be edible were being used in the Mesolithic period without hard, tangible evidence like those hazelnuts. But what we can say is that it is possible that they would have been used. They were edible, they could be used for food, and if they were they could have been a very important part of the diet. Now it's a complicated subject to address, because sadly what is edible isn't necessary a black-and-white issue. There are some plants that one can say are definitely edible, for example burdock root. At the other end of the scale one can say that deadly nightshade is definitely a poisonous plant. But it's the area in between which is sometimes the most important. There are plants that are poisonous that may have been made edible. There are plants that may not have been palatable or particularly healthy, but in times of famine would have been really important sources of food. In between the absolutes there is a sliding scale of edibility – in times of famine people will start to use foods that at other times they would avoid because they are difficult to process or because they are not palatable. In fact, you don't have to go back to the Mesolithic period to see evidence of this. There is plenty of evidence surviving in our written history. For example, the potato famine in Ireland forced people to rely upon the wild arum, 'lords and ladies' for food, and more recently, in the Bosnian conflict, people were selling stinging nettles in the markets. When they ran out of these plants they had to start looking for other foods. This is to say nothing of what people did during the siege of Leningrad and at other times during the Second World War. So this sliding scale of edibility presents a problem in some ways. Of course, it may have been that these times of famine led our early ancestors to experiment with processing techniques that enabled them to overcome some of the toxins that plants use to defend themselves from predation by other creatures. One of the fascinating things, when we're looking at poisonous plants, is that sometimes we're dealing with poisons that may go back to a time when the plants were defending themselves against dinosaurs. Plants have been around a lot longer than we have. For example, in black bryony there are raphides, strong, very long, sharp bundles of crystals of calcium oxalate that would be lethal for anything grazing on this plant today. We'll never know what was attempting to eat this plant, but in its evolutionary past it evolved a complicated defence mechanism to ensure its own survival.

Cultural heritage

The last thing we had to do in searching for clues to the past was to look at existing indigenous cultures around the world. I have been very fortunate to have travelled to many parts of the world and have observed how hunter-gatherers interact with their plant resources today, garnering a knowledge that is rapidly being lost. We needed to see how people go about things, investigate their mentality, their psyche and their cultural involvement with plants. Of particular importance, for several reasons, was the way Australian Aboriginals use plants. These people are important, first, because we can communicate very easily with them – they speak English to a large extent. Second, their cultural knowledge is very strongly intact in the areas we would visit and they still regard it as extremely important. Third, they have a very strong cultural connection to their wild foods, something I was keen to explore as it may have been the case here too, although we can't prove it. Finally, they traditionally cook (and that means up until recently) without the use of metal cooking pots, which is exactly the situation of our Mesolithic ancestors – they had no solid vessels in which to cook foods. Our own experiments with processing wild foods – and detoxification in particluar – have allowed us to explore a range of plants never recorded as having been used.

An electron microscope picture of black bryony showing the sharp bundles of calcium oxalate.

A Foot in
Both Worlds

A foot in both worlds

Australian Aboriginals have a very different mindset to the modern Western view of the world. They have their traditional view of the world order and how everything came about, and they also understand Western culture; having a foot in both worlds is problematic for them. Modern Australia still struggles to grasp the subtleties and complexities of Aboriginal culture.

I've spent more time with Aboriginal Australians than I have with European Australians, and I feel very privileged to have had that experience. They have a beautiful view of the world. It's one that places huge responsibility upon the individual to interact with the environment in a beneficial and non-damaging way. Aboriginal people are traditional owners, in the sense that they are entrusted with the caretaking of songs and stories relating to the origin of the landscape and the plants and animals that exist there today. By being custodians of this knowledge they are duty bound to look after the land in both a physical and a spiritual way. We poorly describe this part of Aboriginal culture as the Dreamtime. It's an inadequate concept for a very subtle and complicated world-view, one that reaches to the core of Aboriginal philosophy.

For Aboriginal people in rural Australia, looking for food is obviously a little different to looking for food in Britain. In Britain we can more easily target the habitats and tie in our exploitation of a resource in one habitat with a particular season. The Australian bush is a huge place, and it's more uneven in terms of things coming into season and ripening. You can have a patch of one food resource ripe in one place while it isn't in another. It's a mosaic, and it requires a very high degree of sophistication on the part

(Previous page) Walpiri women dancing the story of a wild frog in the desert. These stories contain the traditional love of the foods – they're very ancient and a vital cultural continuum linking the people with the land. Right: a dance in Arnhem Land, the Magpie Goose dance. The young men are modern Australians in every sense yet confident in the strength of their own cultural identity.

of the Aboriginal hunter-gatherer to position himself in the right place at the right time.

This type of knowledge has been acquired over tens of thousands of years, from observing and listening to their ancestors, and you see that knowledge still alive today. They're rightly proud of that cultural heritage and of their food resources. Although we may laugh in the West at the thought of eating a witchetty grub, an Aboriginal person would not. Only the man who could go into the desert and survive without having to use Aboriginal knowledge would dare laugh at their knowledge.

Almost every food they are involved with has a song, a dance and a ceremony attached to it and is accorded great importance. When Aboriginal women travel through the desert they sing the songs associated with the stories of the land they are passing through, and when they are looking for a particular resource they will sing the song of that resource. So they may be singing the song of the bush potato, and when they find it they will praise the plant with the song. Then they'll dig it up and follow the traditional practices associated with it. Their knowledge of the plants is, as you would expect, incredibly sophisticated. They are real specialists. They know exactly which stem is worth digging up and which is not, and very often the knowledge they exhibit in the way they do things is not obvious even to a scholar of botany. The bush potato is a classic example. From the main plant you get side-suckering shoots and at the base of these you find the edible roots. Very often the roots go much deeper underground than you would imagine. The women know when to intercept a food at the perfect moment, or, at a glance, determine which part of the plant is worth exploiting and which is not. It is a specialist gatherer's knowledge, and we must assume that this knowledge existed here in Britain too. Part of the work we have had to undertake on this project is to try to come to a similar understanding without any guidance or starting point.

Another example of the sophistication of the Aboriginal gatherer, knowledge concerns a root that is used to find water, the desert kurrajong. This tree has a swollen root, and you can determine where the swollen root is because the ground above it is cracked. But you wouldn't imagine that you have to dig down to a metre and a half to get to it. You wouldn't think it physically possible, but they know that is the case. There is a bush food in the desert called the bush coconut, which is a gall that grows on a tree. The gall is caused by a grub, but the gatherers know you have to look right into the centre of the flattened end of this gall to see the head of

Long yams and cheeky yams washed, with sedge and paper bark ready for cooking in a hot termite mound.

Women with wild yams – long and cheeky. The women collect these from the same location their grandmothers showed them, and their grandmothers before them, and so on ad infinitum.

the grub: a little shiny button, tiny, less than a millimetre in diameter – only through such observation do they know that that gall is worth opening because there's a healthy, edible grub inside.

From our time with the Aboriginal communities it was obvious that the roles of the sexes are very strongly defined in Aboriginal cultures. The men really specialise in hunting, and the women principally focus on gathering. As young boys, the males travel with the women, and they obviously absorb a lot of knowledge. But when they come of age, the men traditionally become hunters, and they turn their back on the women's food. Even in a period of starvation they may well still resist eating women's food – it represents women's knowledge, and is not appropriate for a man.

It's difficult to generalise, but I think the future for Aboriginal people is very good. We're talking about a big continent with many different nations who speak many different languages. Just in Ramingining, where we worked in Arnhem Land, sixteen languages are spoken, which gives some idea of the diversity. How many languages were spoken in Mesolithic Britain we'll never know. The future for those Australian Aboriginals who still have access to their tribal homelands, who maintain their connection with the land, is bright because they see themselves as modern Australians but are also keeping intact their traditional knowledge.

A tale of two communities

In Australia we worked with two different Aboriginal communities. First, with the Warlpiri people, who took us out into the Tanami Desert and introduced us to the bush potato, the bush tomato and the bush raisin. They were very gracious in sharing the dances and ceremonies associated with these foods. It was fascinating to hear the short but incredibly moving songs associated with each of these food resources. The dances mimicked the action of collecting and digging each item. So the songs and the dances are in their own right a catalogue of what must be done with the plants.

Their cultural heritage is bound up in these stories – what the ancestors did and what they still do today. In their society the elders determine how to use the resources and specify how it was done by their ancestors. There is a continuum in these activities. I've noticed many times that the elders use their hands in a way that is strange to us. When they show you the right way to do something you quickly realise you are observing a phenomenon that stretches back through time. It's really something to behold.

In the late 1970s there was a huge amount of migration among the Warlpiri from the desert to the cities. It was a complicated process, but often it was precipitated by the need to be near the clinic or hospital in town. In their tradition family members have a duty of care to sick relatives, and it was easier for families to uphold this tradition by moving into town. Like many Aboriginal communities, the Warlpiri are now based in town, and they don't have the free access to wild foods that they enjoyed in the past.

Consequently their diet now involves a lot of white, processed flour, which they cook into dampers using exactly the same cooking process that they use with flour made from wild seeds, but with a fraction of the nutritional benefit. As hunter-gatherers for whom calorific value is always a consideration, sweet things are a prized part of their diet – wild honey is tremendously important in their traditional diet. But ancient instincts based on 60,000 years of hunter-gatherer food culture are now faced with the surfeit of sweet, nutritionally empty foods that the modern urban diet readily offers. Once they have migrated to the city, the diet adopted by Aboriginal communities is often appalling. In some ways this is a microcosm of what is happening to our society as a whole: the Aboriginals have gone from a hunter-gatherer (virtually a Stone Age) society to one consuming a modern diet consisting of many processed foods in under two hundred years. There are massive problems with diabetes, coronary conditions and obesity, problems that exist with other indigenous groups around the world, which also have an instinctive desire for plentiful fat and sugar, and so are tempted by easily processed foods. It's easier to buy a tin of flour than it is to collect and process wild seed for flour.

Both the Aboriginal communities we met are aware of this, and they're glad to go out into the desert when they can because it means they eat bush foods, which they know are good for them. One method that the communities use to deal with diabetes and problems of this nature is to send people back out into the land, to their tribal territories, to have the opportunity to detoxify by eating wild foods. I was struck by the frankness, honesty and deep understanding with which these communities have reacted to the problems they face today. This is something I think has evolved and improved over the last ten years, from when I first worked with Aboriginal communities.

Grandmother and granddaughter – knowledge passing between generations is a time-honoured tradition.

Weaving a dolly bag from pardanus fibres. These bags play
a vital part in food gathering and processing.

The second area we went to was Arnhem Land, in the very north of Australia. The nearest most tourists get to Arnhem Land is when they visit Kakadu National Park, to the west. Arnhem Land is a large area of Aboriginal territory. Currently you have to seek permission and be granted a permit from the Aboriginal owners to enter it. Because of this control over their territory, their traditions and their way of life have been well preserved, and while it's true they do eat a lot of tinned food – corned beef is the classic Aboriginal meat today – they still eat a lot of wild food, and their traditional use of bush foods is still very evident, and is reflected in the health of the people there. They are slim, healthy and active people, in marked contrast to what we observed in the desert among the Warlpiri. Here we worked with a group of Yolngu people outside Ramingining, and we were looking particularly at the way they use one particular plant, a type of yam. It was interesting because we only have one yam in Britain, and that is black bryony, *Tamus communis*, from the Dioscoreaceae (yam) family. Our yam is poisonous. In Arnhem Land, they use two yams – the long yam and the cheeky yam. The long yam you can eat raw, but the cheeky yam is toxic. It contains a similar chemical to the British yam, calcium oxalate. They process it to make it edible, and I wanted to observe in more detail exactly how they do this.

The first thing you notice is how good they are with their eyes, and their skill at spotting the plant. For a start it is camouflaged in the bush, and the season when they're searching for it is the time in the plant's cycle when the leaves are at their most withered and about to fall off the vine, making it very difficult to discern. But if you watch where they're looking you begin to understand. They take in very fine details at a glance. Once the plant has been spotted, they follow the vine down to the ground, where they will then dig down and expose the root. When they find the long yam, the tradition is to cut off the top but leave part of it

Even from a young age children are encouraged to be self-sufficient and to look for food – this is a 'yabby', a freshwater crayfish.

Next page: the cheeky-yam gratings are put in a dolly bag which is soaked overnight to remove the toxins. Salt-water crocodiles lurk in exactly this habitat.

45

attached to the growing stem and replant this, so that the root will grow again.

In the past when I've travelled in Arnhem Land with women who are collecting large quantities of yam to take back to their communities for food, I've noticed that the patch they were going to had been well cultivated by the digging stick. Perhaps this was done to soften the ground and lead to an increased yield. But they may have been digging up the same plant for thousands of years. I often wonder about some of the edible plants in Britain. When we collect nettles from a particular patch of land that's never been put under the plough, are we collecting plants from a source that our hunter-gatherer ancestors exploited thousands of years ago?

The cheeky yam is found alongside the long yam in the same habitat, but it's more round and it has a hairy exterior. Just as with our root, which also has a hairy exterior, it would seem that the hairs that contain the calcium oxalate, which causes a blistering, burning sensation in the mouth, evolved to protect the root itself. So if anything tried to dig it up, it would come to these hairs first and would be deterred by a strong, mouth-burning chemical.

Detox

The way they process both types of yam is quite complicated. They light a fire and put hard lumps from a termite mound – they call it an 'ant bed' – on top; these hold the heat well. While this is heating up, they take the roots to the river and clean the mud from them. Next they collect some sedge from the river.

When the fire has burned down, they move the embers out and cover the hot 'coals', the lumps of termite mound, with a layer of sedge. Finally they put the roots on top of this, clearly differentiating between the cheeky yam and the long yam so they are easy to find

Cooking yams: notice how attentively they observe and learn from skills practised by an elder, and so learning is carried down the generations.

afterwards. Then they place more sedge and bark on top of this before the whole thing is sealed with soil and left for two hours to cook. While it's cooking they go to the river and cast great big hooks with worms on them, hooks no European fisherman would think of using in such circumstances, and reel in little fish and crayfish. During our time with the Yolngu I noticed that they are constantly searching for food. They can be nattering and laughing and yet they are also food-gathering simultaneously. This is something I think would have been the case here in Britain, too.

Once the food has cooked for two hours, they open up the ground oven and separate the two roots, with the long yams eaten there and then. They're delicious: the creamy-coloured root tastes like potato, wonderful and very sustaining. The cheeky yam is now peeled, and what's left also looks similar to a well-boiled potato – it's soft and pulpy on the outside, a little floury and sticky, and yellow. Next they put a digging stick in the ground pointing up at a 45-degree angle. Using a snail shell with a small hole made in it for the purpose, the cooked cheeky yams are now grated. The gratings are then taken and put in an open-weave dolly-bag, which is immersed in the water of a billabong, or small stream, and left overnight to help the toxins leach out – indeed, you can see a milky substance leaking out when it goes into the water.

The following morning the peelings are safe to eat. They're delicious and nutritious; you take these little shavings and press them into a ball in your hand. The cheeky yam has a much higher calorific content than the long yam, which is why they go to all this effort. Without a laboratory to tell them, they knew. Just by the taste of something and the way they feel about it, they can discern that something has more food value. If the Yolngu can do that, then we too should be able to do it instinctively. And that was something that would be important to us later on in the project.

Michael with a guana. This means more than just food. Michael shares a kinship with the guana which brings both benefit and responsibility – he has to look after the welfare of guana in his country. The elder looks on in the background as the traditions are continued.

Foraging

Sea buckthorn – much more abundant in the Mesolithic, a nutrient-rich food of great importance.

foraging

A key point to understand about the way our ancestors lived from the land is that there were available to them a lot of sources of food that required very little effort to gather – things they could pick up with their hands, or dig up, or collect without any specialised tools. This is something I have particularly noticed while working with indigenous groups in other parts of the world. Sometimes it can be quite shocking, because our modern sensibility to food is shaped by the fact that all our foodstuffs are processed and come from shops.

A few years ago, when I was working with a group of people in Venezuela, we were out in the forest and the local hunters had brought with them manioc bread. There was a short wait while the camera was being set up, and the local guys were a little hungry. They got out the manioc bread and tore off sections – it's rather like a giant pizza – and passed these to each other. As one man munched away, it became clear that he was a bit disgruntled that it was just manioc bread, and that he wanted to add something to it. Without any fuss at all, he took his machete, dug into the ground, pulled up a handful of earthworms and made an impromptu live-worm sandwich, which was quite horrifying to watch. But when you think about it, how incredibly practical. He was adding protein to his diet for the expenditure of less than one calorie. It's exactly those sorts of foraging habits that we have to consider as having been possible in the Mesolithic period. There's no evidence of our ancestors eating worms, but that isn't to say that it didn't happen.

Birds' eggs

There are an awful lot of things that we can collect in the countryside for food. Many things today are protected by legislation, however, and therefore we are not allowed to collect them: for example, birds' eggs. Birds' eggs would have been a classic source of food for our ancestors, particularly pigeons' eggs. Pigeons have broods throughout the year – even late in September you can still find pigeons laying eggs. In season, wild geese coming to this country to breed would have been a good food source. Ducks and other birds that raise their young not in trees but on the ground, perhaps in reed beds, would be a potential food source for a forager, who might easily just stumble across a nest.

It's highly likely that our ancestors would have used these readily available food sources. They may have eaten the eggs raw, but there are two very good ways to cook wild birds' eggs. One is to wrap them in moss and put them on the fire – when the eggs are steamed hard you hear a popping sound and if you break the egg you will find it's hard-boiled. Another method is to make quite a wide hole in the top of the egg (in the case of a goose egg it needs to be about a centimetre wide), place the egg in some embers to one side of the fire and let it cook slowly. If it cooks too fast, the hole can reseal and the egg might explode. You don't want to end up with an eggy face! If done correctly, the egg cooks slowly and you get a lovely hard-boiled effect. It tastes different to an ordinary hard-boiled egg because the smoke from the fire permeates the egg. Delicious.

Insects and grubs

Other things that may be harvested in the countryside are various insects and grubs that again our ancestors may have encountered. There's a grub, a white maggot about an inch long, found among the stems of cat's-tail, or great reed-mace, and in rotting logs you can find the larvae of various beetles, which are also edible. Whether our ancestors did eat these things we'll never know.

Wood-ant nests can be broken open and the ants encouraged to gather together the larvae and pupae they are protecting inside their great domed nests of needles. These make very good eating. In some parts of northern Europe these are still commonly harvested and used today, particularly for feeding to chickens, because they make for a very enriched egg yolk. When handling a wood-ant nest, you need to be cautious because the ants can defend themselves by squirting formic acid at you. If you tap the nest with a stick, they will squirt the stick with acid, making it smell like vinegar. It's almost an asphyxiating odour. On a summer's day, if you take a white or light pink flower and throw it on to the nest, then tap the nest, when the formic acid is dispersed the flower will change colour, like litmus paper, to a purply shade. Children are fascinated by this.

Amphibians

Frogs must have been used as a source of food, and probably toads as well, although toads have glands behind the eyes called paratoid glands which are toxic, and potentially also toxic internal organs. Toads were definitely part of the British diet at the turn of the twentieth century. The use of toads' legs to make toad pie is beautifully described in *Lark Rise to Candleford*. And of course, our cousins across the channel in France are greatly fond of frogs' legs.

Farther afield, in the rainforest, frogs are very widely collected. In central Africa, particularly on rainy nights, people will go out with buckets and collect large quantities of frogs to cook, and it's hard to imagine that members of the Rana genus wouldn't have been used in this country. They make good eating. Of course, today all amphibians are protected by law in Britain, and rightly so.

Honey was the only source of sweetness for our ancestors as it is for the Hadza today and they would go to great personal risk to obtain it.

Reptiles

Although they may have been eaten here, our snakes are really too small – we don't have the large, fleshy snakes that you find in other parts of the world. Thick snakes, although a bit bony, can make for good eating.

Snails

A common sight on some parts of the chalk downs is the large white Roman snail. Apparently these were introduced by the Romans in order to be farmed for food. But our common snail, the grey snail, is also equally good eating, and is easily gathered. When I was younger, travelling along the North Downs, I'd often cook snails. I'd pick them from the grass in the morning and put them into the embers of the fire with the shell opening facing upwards until they bubbled furiously, at which point they are cooked. They are a little chewy, but they have a pleasant taste. The only thing you have to be careful of with snails is to ensure that they haven't been eating anything toxic. Don't collect them if they're close to woody or deadly nightshade, because they can concentrate the toxins from these plants in their flesh. When they're used commercially, they are fed on bland, safe foods such as dandelion leaves, or even garlic to impart a flavour before they are used in the kitchen.

Crayfish

In our rivers today there is a battle raging between the invading crayfish from America and our smaller, native crayfish. The invaders are forcing out our native crayfish. They have also brought with them a disease that kills our native crayfish, which is a great pity. Our native species has been in decline for a long while, but it was certainly a useful food source for our ancestors, I have no doubt about that.

In some parts of Britain it is legal for you to collect the invading crayfish, which are as big as a langoustine. They can actually be picked up in a clear-flowing chalk stream by hand, or are easily speared. They're normally gathered using a trap baited with fish remains, which lures the crayfish in, particularly in darkness. It is possible to collect hundreds, if not thousands, easily; such is the extent of the problem with the foreign invaders today.

American crayfish, an alien invader in our waterways but too good a wild food to pass by. They are hard to kill, but I don't like to cook them alive so I cut across the spinal cord just behind the head (top left). Then you break the central blade of the tail, pulling it to one side until it clicks (top right), and then back the other way until it clicks again, and finally pulling it out. This should take the alimentary canal with it, and so clean the crayfish. The hole that's left is a good place to put a skewer so that you can hold the crayfish beside the fire (bottom left). Cook them until they are scarlet or bright orange – delicious! (bottom right) Some of the American crayfish have as much meat in their claws as they do in their tails.

Coastal foods

One of my fondest memories of working with Aboriginal people is from 1996 when I first stayed with Australian Aboriginal people and we worked with an old man and his wife and family. Towards the end of our filming he decided he would take us on to the shoreline to search for mud crabs. This wonderful gentleman would locate a hole that would be ideal for a mud crab, poke around in it with a hook he had for pulling the crabs out of holes, but repeatedly find nothing. Each time this happened, a few moments later his wife, who had been walking along behind him, would reach into the same hole with her fingers and pull out a crab that he had missed. It was wonderful to watch, and there was a lovely display of family dynamics going on. At the end of the day, as the sun was setting, we sat beside a fire and cooked the crabs together. There were a few crabs left over, which the wife wrapped up in a leaf and gave to me.

It was a wonderful scene to be part of, and I often think back to that time when I'm on the coast of Britain. Sometimes, when I see a family with their wellington boots and fleeces on in the winter playing in rock pools, I try to imagine what it would have been like thousands of years ago. As a family they may have moved along the shoreline, perhaps relying on a network of shelters all a day's walk apart. The family might have with them a sea trout they had caught in the estuary they had left a few days before, as they made their way up the coastline. They would have timed their journey with the low tides at the beaches. And there, standing by the shore with the wind tugging their long hair, they would wait for the tide to go out, ready to advance behind it, their stomachs hungry. When the tide closed again over the beach they would be happy in the knowledge that they'd got a few limpets inside them, able to move on again, the children laughing and giggling, being warned to be careful on the slippery rocks, just as they are today.

I often quote the Native Canadian who said, 'When the tide is out, the table is set.' You need to understand the tides, so there is a real art to collecting food from the coast. The last thing you want to do is to get caught out by the tide coming back in. Our ancestors who lived on the coast would have been keenly attuned to tide changes without the benefits of a timetable. They would simply have learned from experience, just as people who live on the coast do today.

But although when the tide is out the table is set, it's not set for very long, so you need to have a good idea of where you might find each resource.

Seaweeds

Seaweeds are very important as a source of food. They're very rich in nutrients, almost the perfect food. There are some plants called sea sorrels, genus Desmarestia, which are toxic, too acidic for consumption, but other than this all our seaweeds are edible. Because they are so rich in nutrients you shouldn't eat them in large quantities - they may have a strong purgative, or even emetic, effect. Kelp has everything we need for life within it. It's quite an astonishing material, and it's hard to imagine our ancestors not making great use of seaweed. My own preferences are for the softer seaweeds, particularly a beautiful pink seaweed and a sea lettuce, both of which you find growing abundantly in the summer, along with carrageen.

Limpets

We know from archaeological records that our ancestors spent an awful lot of time by the coast during the Mesolithic period. Our hunter-gatherers relied heavily on coastal resources. Much evidence has been found of the presence of Mesolithic communities on the coast, particularly midden mounds. The mounds have been excavated often to a depth of many metres, representing hundreds and hundreds of years of occupation and exploitation of the same resources.

The easiest things to gather on the coast are the shellfish that are exposed at low tide. One of the food resources that we don't really use today, but which was probably the most important shellfish resource of the Mesolithic era, is the common limpet. Unimaginable quantities of limpet shells – hundreds of tons – cooked by our ancestors have been found in midden mounds. Limpets were struck from the rocks with a small hammer made of a narrow piece of stone averaging about 15 centimetres in length. The limpet knows that you're creeping up on it. It clamps down

(Overleaf) top left: mussels. Top right: limpets. Centre: razor shells. Bottom left: winkles and whelks.

and you can't get it off without breaking it. The way to cook a limpet is very simple: put it on a rock and cook it very quickly under fast-burning, very thin twigs, or even just straw placed over the top. It only requires a short cooking time because of the high temperature. When it's done you can blow the embers and ash away and the shells just lift off, leaving the limpet, covered with a black blister. So you just peel that black blister. They make for quite tough eating, but they taste good. In the modern kitchen we can use them to make chowder, but even cooked in the aboriginal way they are absolutely delicious – very much a taste of the past. It puzzles me that we don't use them today, even though for our ancestors they were such an important food source. And they're less prone to other problems associated with shellfish toxins, because they don't feed on other creatures, and that makes them a much safer resource to rely upon.

Whelks and winkles

Other univalved shellfish that our ancestors used include whelks and winkles. Some people say that you can't eat dog whelks, but this is not true. They make good eating, and again they can be cooked very quickly in a very light ember fire at a high temperature. After cooking, the problem is how to prise them out of their shells. Interestingly, some of the whelk shells that I've come across from middens have a hole in one end, and I wonder whether the hole was in some way created by our ancestors to break the suction within the shell. In some parts of Central America, little river snails are cooked by boiling, and eaten by removing the breaking off the tip of the shell and sucking the meat out. It's possible that something like this was done with our whelks and winkles. Perhaps we'll never know, or maybe an archaeologist will carry out research in this area.

Mussels

Of course, many of the shells that we find on the coast are bivalves (molluscs with two shells). The classic bivalve is the mussel; these are filter feeders. They live by filtering nutrients from the sea and they pass huge quantities of water through their bodies every day. One of the problems for us is that this method of feeding can concentrate pollutants in their bodies. There are two sources of pollutants. One is human effluent or sewage outpour. Very often you will find good mussel beds close to sewage outpour because they feed from it, and can concentrate within their bodies pathogenic bacteria that can cause humans hygiene issues. The other source of shellfish poison is a marine one – dinoflagellate algae, the so-called red tide algae that can cause various types of shellfish toxicity, the most dangerous of which is parasitic shock poisoning, which causes some people to become paralysed. These algae are largely associated with cold, up-welling currents of water, which can be difficult to predict even today. The authorities use an extract of mussels fed to mice to determine whether or not shellfish beds are safe to harvest. But when there is a problem the authorities will put up signs with an order preventing the collection of seafood at that place for a specified time.

In North America, on the Pacific Coast, when people were suffering from shellfish poison, some of the local tribes would actually post armed guards on the beach to prevent people gathering clams, so there were no more illnesses. Whether that occurred in Britain we can only guess. Fortunately we don't suffer a great deal from these problems.

Farther up the beach there are other mussels to be found on rocky headlands. All we have to do is look for good-sized mussels and prise them off with a rock. Now, with all these bivalves we have to test that they are healthy. We shouldn't harvest any bivalve shellfish that we think is unhealthy. Squeeze the shell open a little and if it's healthy it should clamp closed again. If it opens readily, discard it. Equally, if, after cooking, the shell doesn't open at all, discard it. Before cooking, it's normal to purge shellfish by putting them into clean water, either salt water or fresh water, depending on the species. Fresh water is effective for purging mussels – just leave them in the water overnight and they clean themselves. But when we're cooking in the Mesolithic way in a very hot fire, this is not necessary.

If you're going to use mussels, or any of the clams, including cockles, oysters, sand gapers and scallops, you need to cook them in such a way that the flesh will not fall into the grit of the fire. An extremely good way of going about this is the Aboriginal method of placing the shells in the sand with the hinge upwards, in a nice orderly row so that you can easily find them once the fire has finished. And then, as with the whelks and limpets, build a fast, hot fire over the shells. Because we are cooking the shellfish at temperatures of between 500 and 800 degrees, the bacteria contained within the shellfish are killed more effectively and they are a lot safer than if they had been boiled. To boil them we must cook them for a minimum of twenty minutes at a rolling boil to ensure that all the bacteria inside them have been killed. Our ancestors didn't have cooking pots, so they weren't able to boil them, which probably kept them a lot safer. Also, the shellfish taste a lot better when they've been cooked on a fire.

Razor shells

Each different type of shellfish inhabits a different part of the beach. During the spring tides, the extremely low tides, on sandy beaches in some parts of England we have access to the best of all shellfish, which is the razor shell. They are long, cutthroat-razor-like shells, very common on the beach, although we don't very often see them because they appear only at very low tide. To find them, make your way carefully down on the sand flats and look for little keyhole-shaped holes. Once you've located some, how to get the shellfish out is the real challenge. We know our ancestors ate this species because we've found the shells in their middens, but we've no idea how they collected them. The difficulty is that this type of shellfish can burrow extremely quickly through the sand and can swim through shallow water. It moves vertically through the sand, extending its foot beneath it and pulling itself down.

There are various ways of attempting collection. It's quite astonishing how fast the shellfish goes, so you have to sneak up on it. If it feels the vibrations of your footfall, forget it, it's going to be too late. If you're quick you can reach down into the sand and grasp the shell. You won't be able to pull it out, but hang on to it and then you can dig it out with your other hand. It's a difficult technique and you often lose more than you get. If you have a shovel you can insert it in the sand at an angle to

In New Zealand this style of cooking is still of great importance to the coastal Maori people. Here abalone are cooked in their shells with smoked eel and mussels in a bag made of Pacific kelp.

intercept the razor shell, then get underneath it to prevent it burrowing down and dig it out. But again, it's difficult.

The method I prefer entails using salt (it's unlikely that our ancestors would have had access to salt). Take a teaspoon of salt and place it into the hole, then wait for a few moments and the razor shell will come to the surface. First it pokes the tip of its shell out of the sand, and if you wait for a fraction longer it will come up a little higher and you can see the whole of the shell. Grasp it swiftly and hold on – you will feel it resist you as it fights to get back down into the sand. But after a few moments you can feel it become exhausted and you can easily withdraw it from the sand. It's like magic. Usually the razor shell will then demonstrate for you how its foot works as it flails the air trying to get back into the sand.

Maybe our ancestors used their hands, or maybe they used a stick. Some people in North America use a metal rod with a hook welded on to the end which they drive swiftly into the ground to intercept the foot and the base of the shell, hoiking it out that way. It's quite possible that the same was done here. The likelihood is that we will never know, as one of the great problems with razor shells is that they are very fragile. So although some shell fragments exist within midden mounds, they haven't survived sufficiently intact to permit an analysis to determine whether or not they were cooked, or whether there are any clues as to how they were collected.

They are absolutely delicious cooked in a fire - they taste like crab sticks - probably the tastiest and, particularly when you see how large they can be, the best of our seafood. I rate them extremely highly. Although we don't tend to eat them in Britain (a great shame, but we are overly concerned with the appearance of our food here), in France they are on sale in the markets - even on the streets of Paris you can find razor shells for sale.

Cockles

My next-favourite shellfish are cockles, which I think are one of the most wonderful seafoods. Cockles are found in mudflats at low tide. Where they have been sitting on the surface of the mud they leave a little bubbly shape, so you can determine where they are. Commercial pickers use rakes to harvest them. But you can just rake your fingertips through the mud and expose the cockles. A good-size cockle can be 3 to 4 centimetres across. They are easily gathered and absolutely delicious - a fantastic source of protein when you think how little effort is required to gather them.

Scallops and oysters

Scallops and oysters are not easy to collect from the coastline. Today they are harvested by commercial means, such as trawling or diving. Our ancestors would have been able to find them occasionally trapped in rock pools at low tide. And we know that they used them as a food source because we have found their shells in the midden mounds.

Crustaceans

The coastline is an abundant source of other foods as well. At low tide it is possible to find Scot lobsters - langoustines, as we know them today. Crabs can be found, and also occasionally lobsters as well. And it's clear from evidence in the midden mounds that our ancestors knew how to devise means of trapping these delicious creatures.

You can dispatch lobsters and Scot lobsters by cutting across the central nerve or spine that runs down the back. There's a point on the back of the head in the shape of a cross, and from here you just cut across the width of the body. Then they can be skewered, put beside the fire and cooked in the embers. Crabs need more careful handling. Again, they can be killed by cutting into the central part of the body, through the face, although I'm sure our ancestors didn't bother with that. And they can be cooked in the embers of the fire until they're bright orange in colour. Then the shell is separated from the body and the so-called 'dead man's fingers', the internal parts of the crab, are removed in the way we are accustomed to today. The white meat can be taken from the claws and legs and the brown meat from the sides of the shell.

Hunting

hunting

When we peer through the mists of time into the Mesolithic era, there are so many things we cannot discern, but there is one thing we can say with great certainty, and that is that our ancestors were keen hunters. Just as for the Kalahari bushmen today, hunting would have been a prime concern for the communities of Britain's Mesolithic past. When I travel with hunter-gatherers in Africa, particularly, the hunters want to do nothing more than to demonstrate their ability to go out and bring back meat. It carries a weight in their society that is difficult for us to comprehend today. We come by our meat far too easily to understand the thrill of the hunt, the admiration of the whole community when meat arrives and the satisfaction that it gives to the soul and to the stomach filled with the flesh.

We know that our ancestors were supreme hunters because they've left behind plenty of evidence to support that belief. The most common evidence, of course, is the flint tools and projectile points found in vast numbers from the Mesolithic period. But also we get indications of the hunters' more philosophical attitude to their prey, in the form of teeth that have been pierced or drilled so that they can be worn as pendants or necklaces. In particular I'm referring to the canine teeth from wild boar found in Sweden.

Our ancestors obviously had a huge respect for the animals they hunted, and maybe felt some psychological link with them. Maybe they felt imbued with their spirit when they were hunting. We do know that they had respect for their prey and that they hunted as often as possible.

Previous page: a reconstruction of a Mesolithic fish trap.
Above: it's now a strange sight to see a wolf in a British landscape (this is at a Scottish wildlife park) but it would have once been a common sight.

Mesolithic hunting techniques

Many of the hunting hechniques that our Mesolithic ancestors would have employed will never be known to us. They may have used a variety of traps made from branches or saplings bent over, or with cords made into nooses and snares, but sadly these things have not survived in the archaeological record. Their techniques are unlikely to be represented in graphic records because many of these activities took place away from centres of occupation, in remote corners of the landscape, and employed materials that decayed and returned to nature. From the evidence that does survive, however, we know several things. We know that our ancestors made spears that were fitted with small blades of flint to make composite spear points, the equivalent of a large metal-leaf point spear, with the pieces of flint beautifully glued into the wooden shaft to cause maximum haemorrhage when cast into their prey.

Bow and arrow

Without a doubt the most important hunting tool of the Mesolithic period was the bow and arrow. The bow first makes its appearance in the archaeological record late in the Palaeolithic, but it's in the Mesolithic era that it becomes the dominant force, the most significant tool in the hands of the hunters of that time. We know this from the sheer volume of projectile points we've found in Mesolithic sites – not the elaborate flaked-leaf points or barbed and turned flint arrowheads that come later, but simple, pragmatic blades struck from a central core with a minimum of chipping to fit them to the arrow shaft with a resin glue, perfectly suited to the task. These tools have been fashioned according to the hunter-gatherer principle, maximising their efficiency while minimising the effort of production – easy to repair, light to transport. With these tools, a bow in his hand and a set of sharp flint-tip arrows, our Mesolithic ancestor could delve into the undergrowth of the Mesolithic forest and bring back meat in a way that, until that time, had not been possible. With its reach and accuracy, the bow is a lethally effective tool in comparison to the hand-cast spear (no disrespect to the spear as a hunting tool – it's still widely used in Africa today).

The earliest set of bows to survive from the Mesolithic era comes from Denmark, found at a site called Holmegård. These bows are made from elm, probably witch elm, this being the most suitable for the manufacture of bows. They're short broad bows made from saplings, and having replicated them I know that the design is extremely practical. It's very easy to fashion such a bow using flint tools – a fast, flat shooting bow, perfectly suited for hunting in undergrowth. The arrows' shafts

are made of varied materials but the most commonly used throughout Europe would have been the viburnum species – the wayfaring tree or more likely the guelder rose. The reason for this is that the shafts made of this material are stiff and resist the arched paradox– the flex of the arrow as it leaves the bow - more effectively than those made from other timbers, leading to a more efficient and quieter release of the arrow.

Only in a few tantalising instances do the wooden shafts of the arrows actually survive. Where this occurs we gain some insight into how the arrowheads were fitted to the shafts, and the nature of the nocks, which could give us some indication of the strength of the bows being used by establishing the diameter of the string designed to fit the nock. At a site in, south Sweden, an arrow was found with two microliths attached, glued with birch resin, and this is very interesting because this is a thermoplastic glue, meaning it softens with heat and hardens when cool, thus

Whenever people hunted with bows and arrows great care must have been employed in the manufacturing – this is clear when you look at archaeological finds, and is also demonstrated when watching Kalahari bushmen preparing their poison arrows.

Reconstruction of Mesolithic arrows: the birch resin glue is a thermoplastic. Softened by heating, it is very easy to repair or replace the very supple front blades so typical of the British Mesolithic. I think this suggests a confidence in the minds of the hunter-gatherers of the time.

supplying a very swift and efficient means by which microliths could be attached to the end of the shaft. The point of the arrow is clearly designed to penetrate the hide, but the second microlith, set behind the point, is designed to cause maximum haemorrhaging as the arrow passes into the animal. At another site in Denmark an arrow has survived with the microlith beautifully fitted into the notched end of the arrow shaft and then heavily bound with fibre. So there were several different methods in use for binding arrows in the Mesolithic period.

The bow and arrow is a remarkable weapon. Very easily portable, it enables the hunter to move through the forest and respond very swiftly with a minimum of human movement to disturb the prey. In contrast, using a spear to hunt with requires bringing your arm back before you cast the spear forward, creating a disturbance that can cause the animal to flee and present a less favourable target area. With a bow and arrow the hunter can bring the bow up to the point of draw more quietly and less obtrusively and loose a very fast-flying projectile. A kill is therefore more likely.

What would have happened at the kill site we can only guess, but what I've witnessed among other groups around the world is that it's very common for the hunter to take the liver and to eat that at the kill site, cooked quickly in the embers of the fire. Hunting is an exhausting business. A hunter will track an animal's hoofprints or, if it is injured, its spore – the blood trail – until he catches up with it. Naturally, it's necessary to replenish that energy. There are two traditions that survive. One I've already mentioned – the use of the liver as food. The other is to collect the blood from the animal and to drink that. This is still practised in northern Scandinavia to this day – the blood supplies carbohydrate to the hunter and the liver gives a virtually complete meal.

Hunters and their prey

Meat would have been of huge importance to our ancestors, and from the butchery marks on the bone remains of animals found at various Mesolithic sites we can see how the animals were cut up. It's actually very similar to the way animals are butchered today (although our ancestors used flint tools, of course). Hunters look for natural weak spots – hinges, if you like – in the make-up of the animal, which can be exploited to sever and separate the major joints. Almost certainly the meat would have been preserved by drying, cut into thin strips and hung up on racks and frames with perhaps a small smudge fire of smoke to deter insects until the surface of the meat was dry. It would then be left until it had dried into preservable form.

Commonly found at Mesolithic sites are the remains of dogs, and it's been suggested that at this period in history, if not earlier, our ancestors were already utilising dogs as hunting partners. I think this is likely to be the case because one of the animals very highly prized by our Mesolithic ancestors, judging by the animal remains, was wild boar. Wild boar all over the world are heavily hunted, even to this day, by hunters employing dogs to locate them and bring them to bay prior to their being dispatched. In New Zealand there are still big hunting competitions, which involve hunters using two dogs to find and hold the boar until the hunter catches up with it and dispatches it with a knife. Perhaps a similar process was the tradition in Britain. The interesting thing is that many of the wild boar remains that have been found are of young rather than old animals. This may simply have been a case of logistics, a young, small boar being easier to cook and handle than a fully grown one. Why would wild boar have been so important? I can only assume it was the value of the fatty meat. We live in an age when our sedentary lifestyles make it advisable to avoid sugar and fat, but for our ancestors, who were foraging for their food in the countryside, meat that was rich in fat would have been very highly prized.

Very often I hear people say, 'I don't think I would have liked to have lived back then because I don't like the idea of hunting, I would rather live a vegetarian lifestyle.' Today we are able to be vegetarians if we so choose because we cultivate food and because we can transport foodstuffs widely across the planet, giving us access to various meat-free sources of protein in our modern diet. But for our ancestors this was not a possibility. To live as a vegetarian in Mesolithic Britain would have been impossible. Meat was a vital component of the diet. Moreover, hunting provided more than just food. With the slain animal came a whole range of other important resources: skins that could be turned into clothing; sinews that could be used to sew those clothes together and to make bow strings and snares; bone that could be used to make needles and other very important tools; antlers whose uses ranged from the manufacture of fishing harpoons to tools for digging in the ground.

The hunters' role in a true hunter-gatherer society is tremendously important, and goes beyond their technical skill. It's not surprising that around the world, in the remaining hunter-gatherer societies, the strong spiritual associations that come with hunting remain extremely vibrant. In the rainforests of South America, hunters believe that they must enter the spirit world after a successful hunt to appease the spirit of the animal and explain why they took its life. Many of these societies share a tradition whereby the hunter has a pact with his prey not to over-exploit it as a resource. So conservation principles are often built into the fabric of traditional hunter-gatherer communities, whether by taboo – a strongly-held belief that certain animals cannot be hunted – or by more obvious means. Among Native Canadians who hunt beaver, the numbers taken are strictly regulated with respect for the future of the resource.

What we don't see particularly often in the archaeological record are the remains of small mammals. There are many small creatures that our ancestors may have made use of for food whose remains didn't survive, and I think that for every large animal we know about we must consider that there would have been several small animals that would have been caught and eaten. Certainly, from my own observations in every hunter-gatherer community I've worked in, young boys learning to be hunters will start by hunting small animals, which are not discarded but rather valued as a good resource - snacks, if you like, between the meals provided by the larger animals. For example, among the Hadza in Tanzania, the boys go out with bows and arrows to hunt lizards and bush babies and bring these back while the men are out looking for guinea fowl and the larger game. When the men are unsuccessful in hunting larger game, they too will resort to shooting these small animals to keep starvation at bay, and this is an important part of the learning process.

I've often been surprised by just how small a resource will be used by hunters. I remember observing two Hadza boys watching a bird's nest, which they continued to do for several mornings. Eventually they found a tiny bird, the size of a sparrow, sitting on the eggs. They got beneath the nest and, pulling their bows to full draw (totally unnecessary for such a small bird but this is the way they do things), they shot the bird. It was then taken to the fire, plucked, butchered (using an arrow-head,

The late Paleolithic/early Mesolithic period saw the arrival of the bow and arrow, a superlative hunting tool still widely in use – this is an 'antelope's view' of the Hadza approaching – the arrows have poison tips. Whether poison was used in Britain has yet to be discovered.

not a knife), cooked and then fed to the three boys that morning. This is exactly the sort of thing that may have happened here in Britain during the Mesolithic era. Not something we'd like to see today as we've learnt to love birds and protect them.

Of course, it's fanciful to imagine how life would have been here in Britain all those thousands of years ago. But if I draw on my experiences with other aboriginal groups around the world I can vividly picture a father inviting his son to accompany him on a hunting trip. And his son, whose only aspiration in life is to be a good hunter, realises that this is his opportunity. He proudly takes his bow and his arrows and follows his father away from the community into an area where his father knows that there will be deer. Perhaps it's December, and his father takes him up on to the heathland, where he knows that the bilberry bushes grow. He also knows that at this time, December and January, the deer will be grazing the shoots of the bilberries. The deers' grazing process ensures that there will be bilberries for his wife to come and collect in June and July. But now it's December, and the father and son have deer on their minds. They move quietly, keeping their lips moistened so they can sense the breeze, ensuring they are downwind so their scent is disguised. They slip like shadows through the forest, perhaps taking some soil to dirty their faces and reduce the shine. There's hardly any noise in the forest, just the drumming of a woodpecker on a tree in the distance, as they make their way through the clearings. And there, in among the bilberry stalks, they see the flick of a tail, and the father indicates to the son in sign language 'Over to you'.

Later that day, the mother's face lights up as this young boy brings his first deer back to the village, to the community, and there is plenty of celebration. Not just because there is food on the table, but because a trial of manhood has been passed and the community feels secure – they will have shoes and clothes to wear and thread to sew with because there is another fully-fledged hunter in the community.

We don't know what rituals would have surrounded these hunting activities, but we can guess at them. There is one tantalising clue from the Palaeolithic period that perhaps points at the practice of animal worship. At the remarkable site of Star Carr in Yorkshire a set of deer skulls with the antlers partly attached, although greatly truncated, has been found. Holes have been drilled into the skull cases, suggesting that they were

A timeless treat: wild boar roasting on a spit. We know from archaeology that young boar were frequently hunted for food and pork was considered an important delicacy.

possibly worn as headdresses. Various hypotheses exist as to the purpose of these so-called headdresses. Some have suggested they may have been a disguise to allow the hunter to approach their prey stealthily. There may be some truth in this – I myself have approached deer by mimicking their actions and disguising myself as one of them – but I think it's much more likely that the headdresses were used in some ritual, simply because it seems to make more sense based on practices I've seen elsewhere. They could have been worn in a dance to venerate the red deer that were so important to people at that time.

We'll never know precisely what the findings at Starr Carr mean, but one thing that I've found to be true wherever I go with hunter-gatherers is that they have huge respect for the animals that they hunt. The spirit of the animal is very important to the hunter, and there is a direct relationship between the two. The bushmen of Africa never talk openly of hunting. If they're going hunting the next day, they never say they're going hunting, they say, 'I'm going out tomorrow.' They believe that there is a psychological link between the hunter and his prey, and it's important that the prey doesn't know that the hunter is there. The hunter must appear with surprise on his side. He mustn't allow his thoughts to betray his presence before he begins the hunt. Anyone who has hunted will appreciate this perspective, because even today, with the use of modern firearms, the hunter can still feel the same deep-seated emotions.

It's no longer legal to hunt with the bow in Britain. I'm not sure whether this was a wise piece of legislation or not, because bows are still widely used in other parts of the world to great effect. Bow technology has advanced hugely since the Mesolithic era, and today hunting with the bow in other parts of the world is very effective and extremely accurate. The bow is unquestionably a humane way of dispatching an animal; crucially, an arrow is less likely to cause an injury to anyone else – its range is less than that of a bullet and its velocity is small. If you are going to hunt, however, you have to operate within the confines of the law, which specifies clearly when each species and gender of deer can be hunted, with which type and calibre of bullet and at what velocity it may be fired, so that things are done in the most humane way possible.

Cooking meat in a pit with hot rocks – the pit must be sealed for several hours. A whole deer can be cooked overnight. There is no direct archaeological evidence but pits thought to have been used in this way are frequently encountered.

Cooking methods for hunters

The Evenk reindeer herders in Siberia subsist on a diet composed largely of reindeer and pike, and when they butcher a deer it will feed their small community (you could say their extended family) for a period of about a week. They begin by eating the parts of the animal that are most difficult to preserve (the heart and other bits of offal) and then they move on from there. As to how our ancestors cooked their food, we have very little evidence. I imagine that most of the meat would have been cooked in the flames above the fire. Cooked bones have survived, but little more.

It's also possible that they could have cooked underground, using hot rocks, but we have little evidence of such a process, despite the fact that it's an extremely efficient way for a community to cook. We do have the evidence of holes in the ground lined with stones, ash and charcoal, or charcoal-associated matter, which could well have been ground ovens. If they were used as such, whatever was cooked in them was taken out and eaten and all we're left with is this lined hole in the ground, so we can't prove that the findings demonstrate the use of ground ovens. It's one of the frustrations of the passage of time – the land surface changes and we lose features, important evidence.

There are various ways you can go about cooking underground. My favourite way for cooking meat is simply to build a fire and put rocks in it. Don't choose rocks that contain moisture, which will expand and cause them to burst, or rocks such as flint, which have air pockets within them. Materials like sandstone are perfect. And when the rock is really hot you create a hole in the ground and line it with the superheated rocks. The meat goes straight on to the hot rocks and then more hot rocks are placed on top of the meat, followed by a mat of leaves, and a row of sticks is placed over the top, and the whole thing is enclosed with earth. The meat is then cooked as long as necessary according to its volume and the size of the pit until it is cooked through. The pit is opened and the meat comes out just as though it's come out of a modern oven. Regulating cooking time is something that comes with experience, but when done right the meat is delicious. There are many plant foods that can be cooked in the pit at the same time, particularly root fruits, such as cat's-tail, burdock and other underground storage organs, perfect for cooking in these conditions.

It's also possible to cook certain extra ingredients inside the animal

These ancient harpoons have been decorated, suggesting a psychological link between hunter and prey. We'll never know what that might have been, but such behaviour is commonly encountered in hunter-gatherers today – respect is due from the hunter to his prey. I like to think that is reflected in these tools.

itself. One of the things we experimented with during filming was to cook an eel, stuffed with rock samphire, underground. Rock samphire is a very strongly flavoured wild food and is often served today gently cooked in clarified butter. Eels have a lot of oily fat in them. What we did was to skin the eel, easing the skin back down the body rather like peeling a banana, gutted it and lined it with rock samphire and then brought the skin back up over the eel and tied it in place with a thin strip of lime bark. Next the eel was cooked to one side of the fire with just some ashes and embers over the top. When we opened it up, the meat was beautifully cooked and had stayed within the skin, but the rock samphire was transformed and delicious to eat. We had done all this without using any technology that our ancestors would not have had access to, and so we can imagine that these sorts of processes would have been easily achievable by the Mesolithic people, too.

Fishing

One certainty about the Mesolithic period is that people ate a diet rich in fish. We know this from an analysis of human bone remains. How they caught their fish is another matter, however, and it's another area

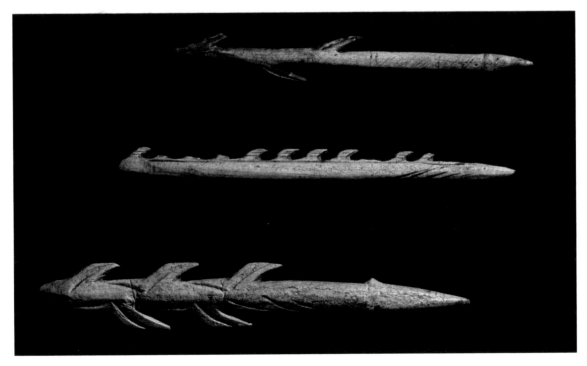

where there's a huge amount of conjecture. We do have some degree of hard evidence. For example, we know that in the earlier stages of the Mesolithic period fish hooks designed to lodge in the throat of fish were in use because they have survived, and there are beautiful bone engravings, sometimes even with a picture of the fish itself.

We also know that fish traps were in use. A few fish traps, woven from willow boughs, have survived from the Mesolithic era. These would have been an extremely effective means of collecting a whole range of different fish. It's likely, judging by the types of fish bones that have been found in coastal middens, that nets were in use, as well as lines and hooks. These could have been trawling nets, or even casting nets, which, used from canoes, may have been very effective in some of our estuaries. Tantalising rolls of birch branch found at Star Carr may well have been used as floats on fishing nets; similar floats were still in use at the turn of the last century in Scandinavia.

One of the most interesting tools from prehistory is the harpoon. Many harpoon points made from beautifully carved antler points have been found from the Palaeolithic into the Mesolithic era, and this is something we wanted to experiment with. In Britain it is difficult to imagine our waterways as they would have been in the Mesolithic era. They have been so altered by the effects of industrial processes and agriculture that in terms of their appearance and the diversity of plants found alongside them they are unrecognisable from those of the Mesolithic period. So we went to the Ardèche, a river that still has a very wild nature, in France. There are still large gravel baths covered in the native flora, and the river is rich in fish life. A huge number of archaeological finds have been made here, including many harpoon points, so it was a suitable place to conduct our experiment.

I replicated some harpoons. I wasn't quite certain how the point would have been attached to the shaft because no harpoon has yet been discovered completely intact. Normally the water of the Archèche would be crystal clear, but unfortunately, for the period of the experiment, it was cloudy because there was rain in the hills. This made fishing very difficult, and I would imagine that in the past our ancestors, in these circumstances, would almost certainly have abandoned their fishing until the water had cleared, because when you can't see obstructions in the water fishing becomes almost futile and a waste of harpoon points.

Venezuela: beating vines to produce fish poison. We do have plants that would be suitable for this in the UK but today this would be considered illegal.

I discovered several things. There are two ways of using a harpoon of this nature. You can thrust it into the water without releasing it, or you can cast it into the water as a spear. I've seen both methods employed in other parts of the world. I've watched Australian Aboriginals using the harpoon with a spear thrower (which I also employed in the Archèche) and I've seen them casting them by hand, at times throwing the harpoon like a javelin, and other times placing an index finger on the tip so that the harpoon is halfway to becoming a throwing device. And in other parts of the world I've seen harpoons just thrust into the water to impale the fish. There was no way I could just thrust my harpoon into the water given the conditions, because it was impossible to see the fish clearly enough for this, so I was forced to cast.

I started by fishing at what I thought would be the most obvious spot, from a rocky outcrop over deep water, and all I managed to do was break one of the spears. My next method was to climb into a canoe and approach the fish so that I could see them at an oblique angle, and then cast the spear. I found this to be extremely effective, and I had no problems with spear damage at all. The last method was to wait for the fish to come into shallow sand baths and impale them by casting the spear so that they were pinned to the sand itself. This was also effective, although I did break one harpoon point on a rock that I didn't know was in the sand. But had I known the area well, as a hunter from that period probably would have done, that could have been avoided. It was a fascinating experiment, and my conclusion was that, if fishing with that type of implement, I would ideally look for sandy conditions and try to impale the fish on the bottom. Of course, today it's illegal to hunt with a spear. We had to obtain all sorts of permissions to make it possible to carry out the experiment.

There are many other ways in which our ancestors could have hunted fish. There are records of poachers in Northumberland in the eighteenth and nineteenth centuries catching fish by using birch bark, burning in the ends of cleft sticks, to attract them to the surface. In the rainforests of Venezuela I've witnessed fish poisoners beating the verola vine to release a milky poison, which is then poured into the river, causing the fish to come to the surface, where they are speared, netted and shot. And I have seen a similar practice carried out in Australia using different poisons.

The question is, could fish poisoning have been used in Britain? Today we have a tree growing in Britain that would lend itself extremely well to that process – the horse chestnut. But unfortunately it wasn't growing in Britain during the Mesolithic era. There are records that walnut bark and walnut husks may have been used for that process. I've never had the opportunity to try it, but it is quite possible that walnut could have been used. There are other possibilities. In those parts of the country where soapwort, *Saponaria officinalis*, grows, it's quite likely that this could have been processed to produce a strong saponin which could have been used as a fish toxin. To say nothing of using the leaves from the silver birch tree, which also contain significant quantities of saponin. Again, it's something that wouldn't leave any trace in the landscape, and we may never know the answer to the question. But we have to consider that poisoning was a possibility.

One of the simplest ways of catching fish, which is now completely illegal – a bit odd really, because it's in no way cruel – is called tickling. For generations, country children in Britain would learn to tickle trout and I'm very lucky to be one of the last generations in the country to have experienced it. Simply lifting fish from the water with your hands is almost certainly something that would have been common knowledge among our ancestors.

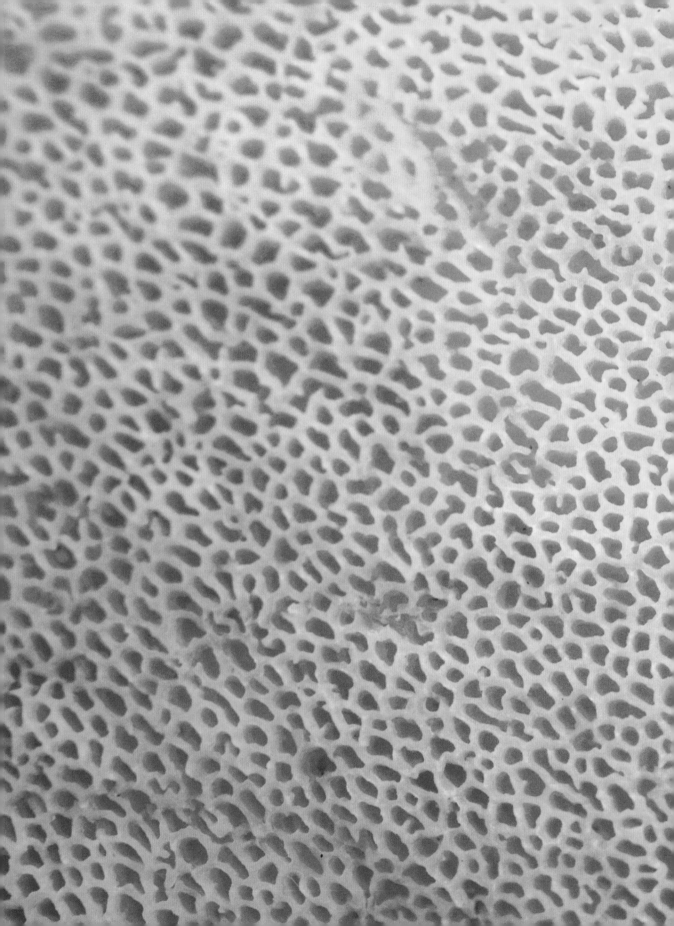

Fungi

fungi

People all over the world have been using fungi for thousands of years. In Britain we've now become rather 'fungi-phobic' and afraid of being poisoned, but there are many parts of Europe where harvesting fungi from the wild is still a celebrated rural pastime in the late summer and autumn. Indeed, it's not difficult to imagine how important fungi would have been to our British ancestors, who must have found them a wonderfully tasty supplement to their other foods. As the climate was so much wetter, and fungi thrive where it's damp, it's likely that certain types of fungi would have been very abundant.

Boletus family.

One of the greatest difficulties of learning about wild fungi is the massive variety and subtle differences that exist even within individual species. It's confusing even for experienced mycologists. In the thirty or so years I've enjoyed collecting mushrooms in the wild the names of the fungi, their classification and their descriptions have changed greatly. Increased understanding of their genetic constitution has enabled mycologists to make differentiations between individual varieties. I'm not sure it has always helped the study of fungi to change the names of species when perhaps it would have been better to keep the names that had been used for twenty or more years.

The key point is that it's a difficult area and one where it's essential to seek professional advice before venturing out into the field. The old saying, 'A little knowledge is a dangerous thing', might have been coined to describe the quest for edible fungi. With this in mind a thorough coverage

Top left: a fungus of the
Bolete family.
Bottom left: penny bun fungus,
Boletus edulis.
Below: hedgehog fungus.

of fungi is beyond the scope of this book, but it's a subject we're determined to return to when we have a chance to do it justice. So what follows is a glimpse of what might have been available to our ancestors – and now to us.

Fungi grow in many places, some from the ground, some from trees. Among those that our ancestors would have found growing from the ground and identifiable by the spongy layer under the cap would have been the boletus family, still prized for their culinary potential. (Many of the mushroom soups available in supermarkets are flavoured with the penny bun fungus, *Boletus edulis*.) Then there's a really interesting group, the so-called hedgehog fungus, which have tiny projections like spines hanging beneath the cap – hence their name. Several of these hedgehog fungi are delicous and I'm sure our ancestors would have eaten them fresh – or dried them by wind or the warmth of a camp fire as an flavoursome food for the winter months.

If you're a novice at collecting fungi, I would advise you to avoid those that grow from the ground but have gills underneath the cap because most of the poisonous fungi fall within this category. However some, like the parasol fungi *Macrolepiota procera*, has gills but makes good eating. Perhaps the most sought after gilled fungus is the chanterelle, *Cantharellus cibarius*, a woodland fungus

Top and right: chanterelle fungus.

that would undoubtedly have been an abundant and much prized food source. You can imagine the delight of a group of Mesolithic foragers if they came upon these golden delicacies.

Given that Mesolithic Britain was so heavily wooded, the edible fungi that grow from trees would surely have attracted the attention of our ancestors. Among this group is the dryad's saddle, which can reach a huge size – I once found one growing on an old ash stump that was more than a metre across.

The most notable omission from the above are field mushrooms, which are easy to misidentify and confuse with a whole range of toxic fungi. I think they're best avoided until the gatherer has a chance to go out in the field with a proper mycologist and really learn to recognise the different details. Our ancestors would have discovered the inedible or lethal fungi by trial and error, then passed the knowledge down orally from generation to generation.

The issue for us in researching this book was to discover not only what fungi grew in Britain in the Mesolithic period but also how they were used. Even more than any other kind of food source, very few archaeological remains have been found to help us. Unless charred – either accidentally or on purpose – there are no remains for us to study because fungi decompose almost without trace. Intriguingly, two of the archaeological finds that do exist show that fungi were not important just as food.

We know from the excavations at Star Carr that horse's hoof fungus, *Fomes fomentarius*, was important in fire-lighting. Evidence shows that the top section was removed and used as tinder. In a wet climate where dry tinder was so scarce, any alternative to the usual sources would have been of huge importance. The other find was in the possessions of the figure known as the 'Ice Man', discovered in a remarkable state of preservation in the ice of a Swiss glacier where he'd died some time around 4,000 BC. When scientists came to examine some items attached to

Dryad's saddle.

his clothing they found two leather thongs had been threaded through holes in some circular fragments. Analysis showed that these fragments appeared to have been cut from birch polypore, a bracket fungus that grows on birch trees. There's been speculation that the Ice Man was carrying these for medicinal purposes, because research has shown that this fungus has antibacterial properties – another example of how our ancestors' knowledge was much more sophisticated than we might have once believed. It comes as no surprise to find that there's a case recorded in eighteenth-century Britain of a man who was going to have his gangrenous leg amputated, but insisted on going to a healer, who effected a cure with badger fat and puffball spores.

Left: horse's hoof fungus.
Below: young puffballs viewed
from above.

The Plant Foods of our
Hunter-Gatherer Ancestors

The plant foods of our hunter-gatherer ancestors

When foraging for wild foods, our ancestors' aim was to get maximum return for the least energy or calorie output. In other words to maximise efficiency and minimise effort. To achieve this, firstly, they got to know the food resource so well that they could choose the perfect moment to gather it, particularly the below-ground parts of a plant. They had to know when plants were going to be in their best condition, which is not that simple as it may involve looking out for the presence of some other indicator – a flower or a leaf bud on another plant that would indicate more accurately than a calendar the actual growing condition of a plant at the time. So as our ancestors had to be tuned in to the right environmental indicators. It was that kind of knowledge that made all the difference for a hunter-gatherer of the past.

They had to know how to recognise the plant at the time they need it, as the properties and appearance of a plant often change as it goes through its annual cycle.

Then, they needed to know the best, most efficient method of gathering the food – what are the soil conditions? What tool do I use? – which, again, our ancestors would have known.

Below-ground – roots

Root foods were an extremely important food source for our ancestors. In Britain we have over 90 indigenous species of edible roots of which most were probably used by the combined populations across the country as a whole. Even an individual band of hunter-gatherers probably used 20-30 species in the course of their annual round. Compare this to our present-day diet, in which root foods are dominated by single introduced species – the potato – and in which our cultivated carrots, turnips, swedea and radishes were probably domesticated in the Mediterranean Basin and introduced into Britain, despite wild forms already being native here.

Our concern is with plants that store food that the plant produced in its foliage during the previous seasons, and which has now moved down into the roots to be stored as starch. Storage roots vary greatly in size

Clusters of tiny tubers of lesser celandine already forming next years shoots in mid-December, East Sussex.

and kind; for example, there are large root systems (tap roots), underground or underwater stems, such as rhizomes, globe-shaped stem tubers like those of the potato, and corms, which are compressed underground stems that grow vertically. The bland taste probably appeals to a lot of palates, in contrast to the broad range of distinctive and often strong flavours offered by wild roots.

Root foods of all kinds are an important energy supply, being rich in carbohydrates in the form of starch. Another advantage is that once dried they last indefinitely, which was particularly useful for hunter-gatherers, as it meant food could be carried with them as they migrated. They just need soaking in water to rehydrate them, before being prepared or cooked just as if they were fresh. The gooey, starchy inner material could also be pounded out in water and allowed to dry to a sort of biscuit, which was more compact, even moretransportable, and widely produced by recent hunter-gatherers.

In the past, root foods represented one of the few foods that were available all year round. Nut foods were only available in the autumn and were difficult to store; some seed foods were also hard to store, particularly in the damp climate of the Mesolithic. Root foods, by contrast, are often self-storing. And, although digging up roots is often energy-demanding, once you've got them out of the ground, there is generally very little effort involved in preparing them to eat, as long as they're not toxic.

However, our hunter-gatherer ancestors sometimes went to what seems to us to be a lot of trouble to make the more unpalatable or even toxic roots safe and good to eat. Techniques such as pounding, grating or leaching the root were used, and it was not un-common to use a combination of some or even all three of these.

In the course of looking for roots to harvest they would have come across those, such as the roots of lesser celandine, that are so tiny that it hardly seems worth your while gathering them. It is often the case, though, that these roots grew in conveniently gatherable clusters belong to plants that grew in great abundance in the Mesolithic era and therefore would have been available to our ancestors in large quantities.

For our ancestors, it was also important to know when root foods were available and at their most energy-rich. Digging up plants speculatively would waste a lot of energy. Since roots can't be seen from above ground, hunter-gatherers would have had to be very well acquainted with the growth cycle of different plants.

Many edible roots are produced by plants that are biennials, so called because they complete their life cycle in just over two years. The cycle starts with the shedding of seed and their germination in late summer or early autumn. In mid or late autumn the plant's seedlings form small leaves and the plant settles down for its first winter, then continues to grow during the next year. By the end of its first full year of growth the plant has formed a big rosette of leaves, and a root full of stored carbohydrate. So from the first autumn through to the following spring, biennial roots are in their prime. If you leave it too long after that, all the goodness from the roots will have been directed into the new second-year shoots. Once the plant begins to form its flower-heads, all the energy from the root has been directed into the above-ground parts and the root is no longer worth harvesting.

There is also a staggering range of perennial root foods available in Britain, particularly in wetlands and coastal zones. Perennial plants live for several years, and many of them produce edible roots that are available year round. During the periods of the year when all the above-ground parts had disappeared, the roots can be difficult to find, so our hunter-gatherer ancestors would have developed systems to mark where the plants grew to make finding the roots easier.

Above-ground – seeds

With the arrival of agriculture and the first farmers in Britain came a dependency on grain foods like cereals; these foods still form a major component of our diets today.

The seed foods eaten by our ancestors were quite different, and, as with other foods, we have little idea of their overall role in diet. Nevertheless, seeds certainly offer particularly concentrated sources of carbohydrate and it is often easy to gather large amounts with little effort compared to digging up deep roots. It's not surprising, therefore, that archaeological remains indicate widespread use during the Mesolithic of seeds such as those of water-lilies, which continued to serve as staples among recent hunter-gatherers of the temperate zones of North America such as the Klamath. Other modern groups such as the Ojibwa were heavily dependent on seeds of wild rice-grass, while other grass seeds provided staples for pastoralist groups such as the Mongols.

On the other hand, the heavy consumption of a broad spectrum of small seeds by Mesolithic hunter-gatherers of the Mediterranean and Near East generally seems to have declined northwards and been replaced by greater consumption of roots and nuts. This may well reflect the high energy input often involved in making small seeds digestible. Unless they're finely ground or cooked as porridge, seeds can travel through the gut intact, which means that their nutrients will not be digested. Another problem lies in parching – toasting seeds until they become brittle and easy to grind. Bigger seeds are easier to parch, but a lot of plants produce seeds in large quantities but of a tiny size and parching them requires some skill as you have to remove them from the heat as soon as the first few crack, otherwise they will char.

Above-ground – rosettes

Some plants survive the winter by producing a rosette of small leaves that grow tight against the ground. These plants would have been of particular value to our ancestors because they provided a ready source of vitamin- and mineral-rich green plant material at an otherwise fairly barren time of year.

Although they are a valuable food source, rosettes can be difficult to identify as they often look very different to the mature plant. Whereas these days we often learn to identify plants by their flowers, hunter-gatherers had to be able to identify plants outside their flowering season. Rosettes can also have very different properties to the mature plant, to the extent that plants that are otherwise virtually inedible can be tasty delicacies during the winter months.

When gathering winter rosettes it would have been important to search in sheltered areas where the leaves survive in a healthier state. Always make sure that you leave the roots of the plant undisturbed, together with a few of the lowest leaves leaves so that the plant can continue to grow.

Above-ground – shoot tips

In early spring, a great variety of tender young shoot tips become available to the forager. With plants such as butcher's broom in which the shoots become bitter as soon as they turn green, cover them over with a layer of dead leaves or earth so they grow without exposure to light. This will keep them pale and minimize their bitterness.

Always look for the thickest, crispest shoot tips – they will be much less fibrous than the thin wiry ones.

Above-ground – seedlings

One of the leafy green foods that our ancestors would have been aware of, but that we hardly ever consider today, are emerging seedlings. Again, these can be vastly different to the mature plant and a keen eye is needed to recognise them. Not all seedlings are edible, however; many are far too bitter to be considered good eating, and some are toxic.

On the whole, you should avoid red or purple leaves and shoots, which often indicates a strong, bitter flavour and a fibrous texture. As a general principle, you should target plants growing in shade or in sheltered surroundings, particularly where it's moist, as these conditions tend to produce larger, milder, more succulent leaves and shoots.

Seedlings worth collecting include those of the honesty plant, beech, sea-kale, hornbeam, charlock and Himalayan balsam.

Above-ground – mature green leaves

Mature green leaves grow in abundance in Britain, and for our ancestors they would have been a vitally important foodstuff. A further general principle to remember when collecting wild leaves is that they also tend to become more bitter once the plant is in flower. If you've found a resource that you will want to use on a regular basis. It is therefore worth cutting-back any shoots which show signs of forming flowers, and indeed older shoots generally. Stinging nettles and chicory are just two of many plants that can be induced to produce new shoots by being cut back in this wasy. The leaves of tufted plants such as dandelion, ribwort plantain, broad-leaved plantain, ladies' mantle and salad burnet also benefit from being cut back, after which they produce new leaves that are larger, milder-flavoured and much more succulent.

A typical clump of sea kale in August, East Sussex.

*Harvesting the green pods of our native species of the everlasting pea (*Lattheris sylvesteris*) in August from a hedgerow near Bignor, Hampshire. These succulent green peas are delicious raw or steamed.*

Above-ground – nuts

Our ancestors would have had easy access to nuts as a food source and would have made good use of them: they are very calorie-rich, being full of carbohydrates and fats. They're rich in protein, so they are a good all-round food and extremely sustaining.

The big problem is digestibility; even the hazelnut, the most digestible of our native nuts, is not easy to digest unless it's cooked, and nuts such as acorns require more elaborate treatment.

Archaeological records suggest that hazelnuts were a staple component of our ancestors' diet. A site on Colonsay has recently given us a pretty good understanding of how our ancestors may have used them. At this remarkable site Professor Steven Mithen and his team found hearth remains and underground pits, which would have functioned as simple ground ovens where hazelnuts were piled and covered to be cooked as explained in Chapter 2.

Among the many plants offering potentially rich caches of nutritious foods, many were highly unpalatable, often indigestible or even toxic. In place of modern cooking methods and adding ingredients such as sugar, our ancestors drew on an extensive repertoire of traditional techniques that were effective in rendering the plants palatable, digestible and safe to eat.

There are four aspects to the way we experience the palatability of foods: sweetness, sourness, bitterness, saltiness and astringency. They can be controlled or manipulated by processing food in different ways.

Sweetness in food is of tremendous importance to human beings. We crave sugar because some of the sugars provide the most easily assimilated form of carbohydrate for the human body. Our brain craves a supply of carbohydrate on a constant basis, so naturally we have evolved with a predilection for sweet, sugary foods. It is important to know, when searching for edible wild foods, that sweetness can be 'hidden' or bound up within the plants, especially in chemicval compunds call 'glycosides'. For example, most of the sugars in the wild fruits of Britain are in this bound form and require cooking, crushing or exposure to frost to release the sugars and make the fruit taste sweet. Sourness is also important, in the sense that a certain level of tartness, or sourness, is needed to balance sweetness so that it's not overwhelming.

Although bitterness is very often a sign that a food is poisonous, moderate levels of bitterness generally present no problem; indeed, they can stimulate digestion.

Astringency, which causes dryness in the mouth, is due to tannins, and these can make food (particularly proteins) less digestible. Crushing the flesh offers a means of immobilizing these tannins - so long as we then allow a 'curing period' of a day or two for the relevant enzymes to get to work on them. Heating can sometimes induce similar changes. Our ancestors probably would have crushed fruits with a pestle and mortar, cooked them with hot rocks in water, and/or frozen them by laying them on mats on the ground to be exposed to the frost, which also sweetens the fruit by releasing the sugars.

Wild plants are protected by various pieces of legislation, notably the Wildlife and Countryside Act 1981. The Botanical Society of the British Isles has produced a very useful and comprehensive *Code of Conduct for the Conservation and Enjoyment of Wild Plants*, accessible at www.bsbi.org.uk.

All the photographs and samples for analysis in this book were taken for the purposes of scientific evaluation of the practices of our hunter-gatherer ancestors. Our aim is to increase the enjoyment, appreciation and awareness of our native plants – you should NOT assume that you are allowed to follow any of the practices described. If in doubt, please consult the BSBI's Code of Conduct.

Plants by family

A selection of some of the food plants likely to have been used by our hunter-gatherer ancestors

The full range of these plants will be explored in detail in a comprehensive field guide that we are currently preparing. Here, we'll not burden you with too much of the scientific detail, and you'll be pleased to know that the editors have turned my lengthy botanical exactitude into concise entries in plain English. Also, we don't include the vast array of food plants with which we have been experimenting over the many years of our project. Instead, the editors have selected what we hope is a more manageable and digestible selection.

Nevertheless, the plant entries are arranged in a standard botanical order that attempts to ensure that related plants that look similar (and often have similar culinary properties) are by-and-large clustered together.

We have also included some more recent arrivals because although not available to our Mesolithic ancestors, they're familiar to people today and provide clues to the ways in which our forebears might have used certain of the native species.

Horsetail Family

Equisetaceae

Wood Horsetail
Equisetum sylvaticum

The wood horsetail is instantly distinguishable from other horsetails by its whorls of side branches, which have delicate secondary branches growing out of them. It is mainly found in the north of the British Isles.

The green parts of the horsetail are poisonous; in fact, the only part of the plant that is definitely edible is the bud at the end of the rhizomes, which starts to swell in early September and achieves its maximum size by late October. Steaming or boiling them avoids them from drying out. Once cooked, the buds have a soft, floury texture, and taste of potato with a hazelnut aftertaste.

Above: wood horsetail, late September, Perthshire.
Right: wood horsetail rhizomes with buds at their tips.
Late September, Perthshire

Above: marsh horsetail - rhizome and bud in late September, Perthshire. Left: marsh horsetail plant with rhizomes buds, late September, Perthshire.

Marsh horsetail

(E. palustre)

This plant is sometimes found growing alongside the wood horsetail, as well as in bogs, fens, marshes and wet heaths, and sometimes in the shadier areas of meadows. This variety has only simple branches, quite a bit longer than those of the wood horsetail. The buds mature much later than wood-horsetail buds; they're only worth gathering from November up until the start of the following spring. They can be cooked in the same way as those of the wood horsetail.

The whitish, spore-producing shoots of the giant horsetail. East Sussex.

Great Horsetail
Equisetum talmateia

This horsetail has its spore-producing cone, on a separate, whitish shoot about 20cm long. It appears in early spring and the tall, green-branched shoots emerge later, growing sometimes to a metre tall, with long, slightly drooping, green branches. They are most commonly found on the banks of ditches and streams and in damp hedgerows. They occur right across the British Isles apart from the east of Scotland.

The buds start pushing their way up to the surface as early as mid-January. They're oval-shaped, and are up to 8cm long and 2.5 to 3cm across. The buds are not pleasant and are possibly poisonous, but the sporagenic vegetative buds taste pleasant. They are small and only produce a relatively small yield, though, so are not really worth the considerable effort involved in gathering them.

The same probably applies to the sporogenic buds of the field horsetail (*E. arvense*). However, it is worth mentioning that the Dena'ina of Alaska use what seem to be the sporogenic tubers of this same horsetail as a food in their raw state. The indigenous enthrographer, Kari, reports the following: "The inland and Iliamna Dena'ina use horsetail tubers as food … The tubers are collected, after the snow melts in the spring, from river banks and in quiet waters where part of the bank has fallen in. They are sweet and juicy then and are much relished as the first fruit of the season. Later on they become dry and hard and are not palatable. The tubers are eaten raw, with or without lard, and are sometimes put in Indian ice cream." Clearly we need to test some populations of the British field horsetail to see if any of them are equally edible and have the same properties. In the meantime, we recommend that you don't try to eat the sporogenic buds of British populations.

Fern Family

Polypodiaceae

Bracken

Pteridium aquilinum

Bracken grows right across the British Isles in great abundance, favouring woods and heathland, particularly in areas of sandy and light soils. It is distinguishable from other ferns by each leaf having several major branches with their own sub-branches, and with leaf-blades attached to the third tier of branching. Another distinguishing feature of bracken is the little spore-producing bodies, sporangia, which are arranged in a line under the curled-over edge of the leaves. Its third distinguishing feature is its long, creeping rhizomes that spread over great distances, allowing the leaves to sprout up some distance from each other. The rhizomes have considerable stores of starch and have been heavily used as a calorific staple in recent times by hunter-gatherer peoples including the Maori of New Zealand and the indigenous peoples of western Washington in America's Pacific Northwest.

However despite digging up the rhizomes of many populations of bracken in several parts of the British Isles we have so far failed to find any with sufficient stores of starch to justify the effort expended, which highlights the importance of detailed local knowledge when foraging for wild foods. It therefore remains uncertain whether bracken could ever have been a staple food.

Crozier (fiddle-head) of bracken, mid-May, East Sussex.

117

From left to right: bracken rhizomes from one square metre, September, Ashdown Forest. Those on the left were processed as described.

Processing bracken rhizomes that had been dried, soaked and roasted. There was barely any starch.

Trying to extract starch from bracken rhizomes by pounding them in water. Late September, Perthshire.

Products of the pounding again with barely any starch.

(Photographs: Annette Stickler)

Scots Pine

Pinus sylvestris

Although there used to be extensive pine forests in Britain, it is now confined mainly to Scotland.

The pollen as food

Pine pollen, unlike the pollen of many other trees. Most pollen is very nutritious and very palatable as long as it is gathered just as the cones are starting to shed. If they are gathered while they're still green, they may well start to go rotten before they have the chance to start shedding. We normally lay the cones on a sieve and store it in a warm place with a large tray or bowl or other receptacle underneath it, thus allowing the cones to shed their pollen through the sieve as they dry out. Once the pollen is completely dry we will box it or put it in jars. Uncooked pollen is impervious and cannot be digested, but cooking bursts the grains makes available their high concentrations of protein and oil.

The tender young leaves as food

As soon as the pollen has been shed, these tender young leaves become available. They are between 1 and 3 cm long and sprout from the shoots that grow out of the top end of the group of male cones. They have a delicious, sweet lemony flavour, and are very good eating. The more mature leaves can be chopped up and made into a very comforting tea, which is particularly good if you've got a chest or gut infection.

Above: deliciously tender young columbine leaves gathered in high summer for salads.
Below: columbine in flower.

Buttercup family

Ranunculaceae

Columbine

Aquilegia vulgaris

Columbine's favoured habitats are woods and damp places on calcareous soils or on fen peat. It is found right across the British Isles, although its distribution tends to be somewhat southerly.

Even in August the newly formed leaves are delicious raw, with a very mild green taste. They're also good steamed, but are very susceptible to mildews, so you should always take only the fresh new leaves.

The roots are toxic and should not be eaten.

Poppy family

Papaveraceae

Yellow-horned poppy
Glaucium flavum

This spectacular poppy, with its large, slightly crumpled yellow flowers and 20cm-long curved pods, grows all round the coasts of Britain on shingle beaches and chalk cliffs. As with all other poppies, the seeds are edible. Harvesting can generally begin in early September when the pods start splitting and shedding their seed in earnest. The yield is generally not huge, but respectable.

The taste of dampers made from these seeds is good apart from a slight bitter aftertaste.

The leaves are not edible. They have a nice succulent texture but a foul bitter taste.

The roots are reputedly poisonous.

Top: the sculptured black seeds inside one of the pods that had to be split by hand.
Middle: the yellow-horned poppy growing on a pebble beach in East Sussex.
Bottom: the harvested pods are allowed to finish ripening and shed their seeds in tightly-woven baskets.

Above: yellow waterlily in high summer.

Waterlily family

Nymphaceae

Yellow Waterlilies

Nuphar spp

Yellow waterlilies, with their large, waxy flowers and oval leaf-pads, are found in various wetland habitats including lakes and slow-flowing rivers. They generally grow in water around 2 metres deep, growing up from large, knobbly rhizomes buried in the mud beneath the water. It is commonly written that both the seeds and the rhizomes are edible, but although the seeds are very tasty, we question the edibility of the rhizomes.

The seeds as food

There is strong evidence from archaeological sites across Europe of yellow-waterlily seeds being cooked and used as food. We also know that the indigenous peoples in North America consumed the seeds extensively, and the best example we have is from the Klamath Indians of Oregon, details recorded by a man called Frederick Coville. The ten-thousand-acre marshland abutting the settlement studied was a remarkable resource, almost solid with yellow waterlilies. The food produced from the lily seeds saw the

Top: capsules approaching maturity in late July, Gloucestershire.
Middle: young capsule sliced open to show the yellow, immature seeds.
Above: capsules mid-way through fermentation, with some remaining intact capsules being broken open.

Top: unripe capsules being broken open.
Middle: fermentation nearing completion. Seeds being washed clean of rotting capsule fragments.
Above: clean seed.

124

Top: dehusked seed now duly winnowed.

Above: grinding the seeds.

Top: a wrap leaf – large leaf of the water dock, fire-wilted and much of the midrib removed.

Middle: ground seed mush ready for wrappng.

Above: wrapped seed mush ready for roasting.

inhabitants through much of the year. They were very careful about dividing the fruits that they gathered according to their state of ripeness, and they prepared food from them in many different ways; they had different names for at least six of the foodstuffs they produced from the seeds. The Klamath used their dugout canoes to harvest the fruit, bringing them back in huge quantities, and used the canoes for much of the processing too. The archaeological sites in Europe which produced yellow waterlily seeds, included a Mesolithic settlement in Denmark, with charred seeds which had probably been cooked for consumption.

The seeds, initially enveloped mucilage float away over the water, and eventually sink and take root. To gather the seeds you need to use a boat. Ideally you should target fruits that are just beginning to split, as you want them as ripe as possible. But to make your fruit-picking trip worthwhile, it makes sense to also gather ones that are slightly less ripe. Traditionally it was common to dig a pit beside the lake or river and let it fill with water, then lower in the fruits in a basket and let them rot. You can of course use a vat instead. The seeds are ripe when they turn from yellow to a buff colour, which takes a minimum of two weeks. Be aware that if you take them out too soon they will taste very bitter indeed. The dried seeds have their coats removed, then winnowed, parched and ground. They are very good eating, with nutrient-rich oils, a respectable quantity of starch, some sugars, and a good volume of protein.

The roots as food

The rhizomes grow in the mud about 2 metres underwater, and are therefore quite a challenge to harvest. It is widely written that the rhizomes can be made edible and palatable by roasting and boiling them, but although we have experimented extensively, the results all proved quite inedible.

There is a North American species, *Nuphar variegatum*, which is apparently more palatable; there are several reports on it being consumed after boiling or roasting in the traditional diets of, amongst others, the Iroquois, the Woods Cree and Nufur species.

The incomparable beauty of a flower of white waterlily with its dense spiral of archaic stamens. Late July, Hampshire

White Waterlily

Nymphaea alba

The leaf-pads of this plant are slightly rounder than those of the yellow lily, and it has huge, delicate flowers with spirals of gleaming white petals and a mass of enormous, pollen-heavy stamens in the centre. Less common than the yellow waterlily, the white species is nevertheless found throughout Britain. It grows in quite deep water, often to 2 or more metres.

127

The seeds as food

Although white-waterlily seeds are less than half the mass of the seeds of the yellow waterlily, they're still pretty big as seeds go. We know that they were used in the Mesolithic period; the site of Mount Sandel in Northern Ireland has produced a good collection of charred seeds and they have also turned up at various other sites in continental Europe.

The seeds have a very similar flavour to those of the yellow waterlily.

The flower buds as food

The buds should be gathered just before the pollen is due to be shed; ideally while they're still closed. The reason for this is that the stamens are full of pollen, which represents the principal source of nutrients, particularly oils and proteins. We normally roast these flower buds in embers and the flavour is, to my taste at least, a bit on the bitter side, but not unbearably so.

Right: a near-ripe capsule of the white water-lily. Early August.

Mustard Family

Brassicaceae (formerly Cruciferae)

This huge family includes the cabbages, kales, turnips, radishes, the mustards, cresses, rockets and shepherd's purse. They are all herbaceous, and even those that are perennial have tops that die back in the winter. They all have the same sort of flowers. The flowers always have free petals and sepals; in other words they're not fused into any sort of tube. Normally four petals, four sepals and the four spreading petals go to make up a cross or a crucifix shape, which gave rise to the old name for the family, 'cruciferae'. There are either six or four stamens.

Many members of this family are edible and have been domesticated, for example watercress, radish, turnip, swede, cabbage, radish, kale, rocket, mustard, and horseradish.

The members of this family also have a lot in common chemically. Most of them contain sulphur glycosides in varying quantities, the highest concentration being in the brassicas, radishes and horseradish. In small quantities, mustards are tasty and stimulating to the digestion. After about a mouthful, though, they become rather acrid and irritating, sometimes enough to blister the skin. Excessive consumption of mustard can irritate the kidneys and lead to iodine deficiency.

Black mustard in early June, getting leggy (1.8 m tall).

Top: overwinter rosette of black mustard in early April, starting to get bushy with plenty of new, tender leaves. Sussex coast.

Above: capsules nearly ripe and ready to shed their round, black seeds that produce a pungent mustard much favoured in the past.

Black Mustard
Brassica nigra

This is now very common in locations across most of England and Wales, particularly around the coasts and on road verges.

Although it is an annual, it germinates in mid summer, and forms a rosette that survives the winter. The leaves are up to 16cm long, coarse, bright green, indented and often very bristly. In the spring the flowering shoots spread and give rise to a diffusely branching superstructure that can reach up to 2 metres tall. The flowers bunch together at the tips, but the fruits spread along the branches. The short-stalked cylindrical capsules are no more than 2cm long, hold the capsules erect and pressed against the stems. There are five or so of the dark reddish-brown seeds in each of the two capsule compartment.

The leaves as food

The rosette's bland-tasting leaves are available throughout the winter but are tough and chewy. By March or early April, however, the new leaves are tender enough to eat raw, and only mildly furry. The flavour is bland with a mildly bitter aftertaste and a slight taste of cabbage. Although there is no mustard flavour, the leaves do make the mouth tingle. The tougher leaves are best steamed or boiled to take away the bitterness, or can be blanched.

The flowers as food

Although they lack any mustard flavour the flowers are good in salads, and if they're still in bud, so much the better. They keep coming well into June.

The seeds as food

The fresh immature seeds can be added to salads, and the mature seeds can be dried in the usual way and used for making mustard.

Charlock

Sinapis arvensis

This is one of our most underrated greens, possibly because it is often thought of merely as a weed of arable land. It is certainly abundant in arable fields, as well as at road verges and on wasteland throughout the British Isles. It has dark-green leaves with a distinctive lobe shape, dark purplish-red leaf veins and bristly undersides to the leaves.

Charlock germinates in late summer and overwinters with a rosette of leaves, but the texture is generally coarse and bristly. Even in spring the quality varies, depending on the soil; on dry soils the plants are small, dark red or purple, coarse and bristly, but on damp soils the plants grow to a metre or more tall with large, smooth, dark-green leaves that are soft and palatable. The leaves have a pleasant mustard flavour and make a good minority component of a mixed salad. Older leaves are better boiled or steamed.

Charlock flowers make an excellent addition to salads. They have a deliciously mustardy flavour that also makes them a first class wayside nibble.

Above left: typical charlock plant on moist soil with tender leaves. Already in flower in early April, East Sussex.

Above right: delicious, tender shoots of charlock in early May. Hailsham, East Sussex.

Below: The delicious flowers gathered ready for a salad.

Above: white mustard is widely naturalised on arable and waste land.

White mustard

Sinapis alba

This plant often escapes cultivation and establishes itself on waste ground and along verges. It has narrower leaf lobes than charlock and long-beaked capsules, the beaks of which are flattened and curved like a sabre. The leaves can be used in much the same way as charlock leaves, although they are a bit stringier and seem to die back rather earlier. The seeds can be used to make mustard, just as they are commercially.

Perennial Wall-Rocket

Diplotaxis tenuifolia

This plant forms large clumps of smallish leaves with narrow lobes, delicate shoots with long-stalked capsules, and yellow flowers. It grows on wasteland and on walls and cliffs across much of England and Wales. The leaves are excellent raw, if bland, and are too tender to cook.

Wall-Rocket

D. muralis

This is an introduced species that is now naturalised across England and Wales. It grows on limestone rocks and walls, arable and waste land, and is similar to the perennial wall-rocket except that this one is a biannual and much smaller. The leaves are tender and have a delicious mustard flavour. However they are delicate and generally so sparse that you won't get much return for your effort.

Left: flowers of the perennial wall-rocket. Early April.
Right: the flowers of the introduced wall-rocket.

Above left: over-wintering leaf-rosettes of sea radish, just above high-tide level, on the coast of County Cork, late December. As so often, one of the rosettes is huge and bushy.
Above right: the immature wild radish, choose green capsules are crisp, succullent and delicious.
Below: young seeding head of wild radish. Perthshire, late September.

Sea Radish
Raphanus maritimus

Sea radish grows round the coast of much of the British Isles. It grows up to about a metre tall and has distinctive leaves, with multiple segments and sharp, serrated edges. In late spring the rosettes produce fine branches and capsules with marked constrictions between each seed.

The leaves are coarse and bristly, with a pungent mustard flavour and a slightly bitter aftertaste. They are excellent chopped up small in salads. You can also add bunches of flowers from the ends of the shoots to salads.

Wild Radish
Raphanus raphanistrum

This straggly-looking annual grows throughout Britain on waysides, waste ground and arable land. It often over-winters quite successfully, sprouts early in spring and the basal leaves are gone before you know it.

However, the immature capsules continue to be available and are fleshy, juicy and quite delicious, as long as you catch them early enough. They are a worthy addition to salads.

Sea-kale
Crambe maritima

Sea-kale looks very much like what it is – a vastly oversized cabbage with huge, flat, leathery leaves, so tough as to be inedible. They have a mass of white flowers that open in late spring and give way to small round fruits like miniature marbles. Sea-kale grows around much of the coast of Britain, except for northern Scotland and the western Republic of Ireland. There are also gaps around other parts of the coast, at least some of which were probably caused by coastal development for housing and sea defences. It is found mainly on pebble beaches and at the bottom of chalk cliffs, and a population of thousands of plants is not unusual along some stretches of beach, particularly on England's south coast.

The leaves as food

Although eating the mature leathery leaves would be, I imagine, like eating rubber sheeting, the very young leaves are edible as long as they're very small, about the size of a child's fist and with the leaf blade still crumpled up. You can blanch the leaves, as Ray does, but personally I quite like the bitterness of unblanched leaves.

The flowering heads as food

The flower-heads are the equivalent of the florets on sprouting broccoli and have something of the same taste; in fact to my mind they have a nicer flavour than broccoli. You need to pick them while the flowers are largely still in bud.

Top: eight year-old Eli gathering the crisp, young leaves of sea-kale. Mid-October, Sussex coast.
Above: while still largely in bud, flowering heads of sea-kale provide a superior version of sprouting broccoli. Early June.

The roots as food

Ethnographic literature generally discusses the use of sea-kale leaves, and sometimes the flowering heads, but very rarely do authors mention the roots. If they do, it's usually to talk about the edibility of other species in other parts of the world. However, the roots of the British sea-kale are also edible and remain crisp and palatable for years. They are at their best in the winter, our ancestors would have can hunted them out by looking out for their big purple buds poking up through the pebbles of the beach and, in many cases, a large number of hibernating snails.

Digging up the whole of the root system is very hard work and is destructive for the plant. A much more ecologically-friendly technique, which also requires less expenditure of energy, is to leave the central tap root intact and undisturbed along with the major root and stem branches, and just harvest food from the surrounding halo of narrow roots.

Although I would personally rather eat the roots raw, cooked by roasting in the fire they do become more digestible. Nutritionally speaking, the roots contain more starch than potatoes, a small amount of protein and a fair quantity of monosaccharides, or simple sugars.

Top: close-up of markers, including hiberbating snails.
Middle: tip of a subterranean stem showing the dense spiral of leaf scars and the purple apical bud. March.
Bottom: excavating a sea-kale root system in early January.

Sea Rocket

Cakile maritima

This plant grows along sandy and shingly beaches all around the British Isles. Its trailing stems carry succulent leaves of the classic rocket shape, and pink flowers.

The leaves should be eaten raw. They have a unique, slightly alkaline, mustard flavour, with a very slight bitterness. If you try cooking them they become unbearably bitter. Probably because the mustard flavour disappears and no longer masks the bitterness. The immature fruits are also exceedingly bitter.

Top: sea rocket growing just above tide-line at Camber, Kent. Early November. Above: harvested leaves.

Above: field cress in early April with overwintering rosettes starting to get bushy – the prime time to step up use of the delicious leaves. Hailsham, East Sussex.

Top right: field-cress in early May. The young flowering shoots are also delicious.

Above right: field cress a week later. The tops of the young fruiting shoots are also edible.

Field Cress or Pepperwort

Lepidium campestre

By early April the over-wintering rosettes are producing a number of leafy shoots. The leaves, eaten raw, are tender and delicious, with a mustardy flavour that becomes milder if cooked. The fresh young shoots are crisp and delicate and can be eaten whole, including the heads of the flower buds. By early May the lower leaves will generally be past their best, but the flower-heads are still delicious.

The mature seeds are well worth gathering around June. They can be ground for mustard, sprinkled whole on salads or added to soups and omelettes.

Other native species of cress, closely related to the field cress, include Smith's cress and the narrow-leaved pepperwort, both of which can be used in exactly the same way as field cress. There are also a number of introduced species that have become widely established in Britain: these have varying degrees of fieriness, and can be used according to taste in roughly the same ways.

Swine Cress

Coronopus squamatus

This small plant grows mainly in southern England and favours waste places, particularly trampled areas like gateways and paths. Trampled plants become 'torped'; that is, small, tough and wiry, and appear inedible, but in moister conditions, they become succulent and large-leaved. By early to mid-April, the leaves are ready to harvest. They are crisp and palatable, with a delicious mustard flavour.

Lesser Swine Cress

Coronopus didymus

This plant is not native, but it has become widely established in many parts of Britain as a weed. On areas of dry ground its leaves are minuscule, and even in those growing in damp places they are still very small. Although the leaves have a pleasant cress-like flavour, they are so small, and the shoots are so wiry and inedible, that it isn't really worth gathering if native swine cress is available.

Above: a relatively succulent leaf-rosette of swine cress.
In mid-April.
Top left: harvested rosette. In early May.
Above left: shoots from a mat of the lesser swine-cress.
In early May.

Hoary Cress or Hoary Pepperwort
Cardaria draba

This is quickly becoming established across Britain. Found on grassy wayside verges, it is recognisable by its frosted-grey foliage and trusses of white flowers. The leaves are very tender, and are excellent eaten raw, with a flavour similar to that of field cress. The youngest flower heads are excellent while they're tightly in bud, and have a more pungent cress flavour than the leaves. They need to be gathered before May, when they generally become too stringy to eat.

Hoary cress in flower in early May.

Shepherd's Purse

Capsella bursa-pastoris

Shepherd's purse is common throughout the British Isles on arable land, waysides and in waste places. It has very distinctive heart-shaped 'purses' (the capsules) with their little 'coins' (the seeds) inside, and a hugely variable leaf shape; the leaves range from being deeply indented all the way to the midrib to just having slightly wavy edges. The flowers are always white. The plant forms over-winter rosettes.

Eaten raw, the leaves are excellent, but they can be rather hairy and slightly bitter, particularly on cultivated land. The tips of the flowering shoots are also excellent as a wayside nibble, but are too chewy to be worth gathering in large quantities.

The plant can also be grown in gardens, under which conditions it generally grows very large with big, tender leaves that are particularly delicious in salads.

Despite being so tiny the seeds can also be used as food. Indeed, they were gathered, roasted, ground and eaten as a 'pinole' or as bread by the Cahuilla of California and by the Chiricahua and Mescalero Apache. For the Mendosino Indians they came to serve as a dietary staple.

Above right: shepherd's purse. Late August with fruiting leaf-rosettes still edible.

Above left: closer shot of flowers and young capsules.

Scury-grass growing at the high-tide line on the coast of County Cork in late December.

Scurvy-grass
Cochlearia officinalis

This fleshy plant has round leaves, white flowers and roundish capsules. It grows round much of the coast of Britain, on muddy or sandy beaches and at the foot of cliffs. It also grows up into the Pennines and mountains of western Scotland.

It enjoys considerable fame as an antiscorbutic; Captain Cook and his crew used it extensively to prevent scurvy on their expeditions to the southern seas. Cook, or more probably the expedition's botanist Sir Joseph Banks, found scurvy-grass growing even around the coast of the islands that make up Tierra del Fuego.

The leaves have a very pungent taste, although not unpleasant.

Danish scurvy-grass
Cochlearia danica

This is a more diminutive species, with very small flowers that range from white to slightly pink, and leaves that are a similar shape to ivy leaves. It's common and often forms huge carpets on sandy and rocky shores, on walls and banks by the sea, and at road verges.

Honesty

Lunaria annua

This elegant purple-flowered plant is becoming a familiar sight in our hedgerows and waysides. It has broad, attenuated leaves and flat, silvery capsules with huge brown discoid seeds.

Honesty is generally a biennial that often overwinters in sheltered locations. The leaves are available for gathering from late summer through to the next spring, and are very succulent and tender, with a delicious mustardy flavour. The flowers, too, have a pleasant pungent taste, and are excellent added to a salad. Something our ancestors would have known, but that today we tend not to consider, is that this plant's seedlings are also edible.

The tap root, produced at the end of the plant's first year of growth, can reach up to between 6 and 10cm long and 1 to 1.5cm wide. It tastes like radish and makes very good eating.

Top right: honesty - succulent, leafy, 2nd-3rd-year flowering shoots in early April. Hedgerow, East Sussex.
Above: tasty seedlings of honesty in mid-March of a very cold spring.
Right: honesty roots in spring.

Above left: horse-radish roots.
Above right: horse-radish thriving on
the Hampshire coast.

Horse-radish

Amoracia rusticana

These plants form huge tussocks of hairless, green coarse leaves, with white flowering shoots and globular capsules. They were introduced into Britain from continental Europe, escaped cultivation and are now found wild throughout England and much of Wales, with a scattering in southern Scotland and in Ireland. They roots, which are used to make horse-radish sauce, are often 5cm or more across at the top and 30 to 60cm long, and are very hard work to exhume.

The leaves as food

Eaten raw, even the youngest leaves are tough, thin and rather polythene-like. Their flavour varies enormously. The leaves of some plants have very little mustard flavour, and are very bitter and not really edible at all unless you boil them for ten minutes. Other are very fiery and chopped-up finely make a good minority addition to salads.

Lady's Smock or Milkmaids

Cardamine pratensis

Lady's smock, another plant that overwinters with a rosette of leaves, is found throughout the British Isles. These winter leaves often have a very few large, round leaflets. Although the rosettes are pungent, they are just about edible in a fiery sort of way, although they're probably best added to salads in small quantities. The spring leaves have an unpleasant oily flavour that makes them quite inedible.

Top: flowers of ladies smock - a delicate beauty, but too pungent to eat.
Right: lady's smock announcing the arrival of spring.
Far right: the small capsule.
Below: a carpet of over-wintering rosettes in shady woodland in early October near Dunkeld, Perthshire.

Wood Bitter-cress

Cardamine flexuosa

This has white flowers and oval leaves. It grows throughout the British Isles in moist, shady places by streams and on damp waysides.

Eaten raw, the leaves are absolutely delicious, with a mild mustard flavour and a freshness that makes them a perfect ingredient for salads.

Below: leaf rosette of wood bitter-cress growing as garden weed in East Sussex, mid-March.

Winter Cress

Barbarea vulgaris

This is a striking plant that grows quite tall, with a mass of rich yellow flowers and dark-green foliage. It can be biennial or perennial and has rosettes that overwinter. There are records of this plant being very heavily used and an important source of greens in times past but we have consistently found the fresh leaves to be bitter, with a very unpleasant oily flavour. However, blanching them improves the flavour, as does boiling them with two changes of water.

Below: a small plant of winter-cress, June, East Sussex.
Top: an over-wintering rosette of winter-cress, in early October, Perthshire.
Above right: pungent, oily-flavoured leaves of winter-cress, harvested near Brighton in November.

Watercress

Rorippa Nasturtium-aquaticum and R. microphylla

Both of these species of watercress grow abundantly throughout Britain, in wetland environments with flowing water. The delicious leaves and young flowering shoots can be used in salads, soups, omelettes and a range of other dishes, but great care must be taken in gathering the plant from the wild. Firstly, no part of the plant should be eaten uncooked if it has come from water containing water snails, and where there is any possibility whatsoever of contamination by sheep or cattle faeces, as in water like this there is a very real threat of the highly damaging liver fluke in its infectious phase. Secondly, it's all too easy to confuse the watercress with the fool's watercress, (*Apium nodiflorum*), especially when there are no flowers, capsules or fruits present. If the plant is in flower, however, the distinction is fairly straightforward. Watercress shoots end in spikes of white flowers with four petals, which give rise to typical mustard-family capsules which in this case is; long and narrow with one or two rows of seeds. By contrast, the fool's watercress, a member of a different family, has its flowers in umbels positioned lower down on the stem opposite the leaves. There are contradictory reports on poisoning by fool's watercress – it doesn't seem to consistently poison people who ingest it. This could well be down to the plant's toxicity varying according to habitat. The most sensible approach is obviously to play it safe and not eat anything that can't be positively identified as watercress from he flowers and/or fruits.

Garlic Mustard
Alliaria petiolata

Garlic mustard plants grow in hedgerows and woodland margins and have upright stems, broad, bluntly serrated leaves, trusses of white flowers, and that rich smell of garlic as you brush by them. The leaves are delicious eaten raw in salads, and although they lose much of their flavour when cooked, they make a good addition to nettle soup. But always pick the leaves immediately before you need them as they wilt very quickly. The seeds make a very fiery, pungent mustard.

Above right: garlic mustard in perfect state for salads, banks of Cuckmere early May.
Below: the capsule with its pungent seeds in August.
Below right: over-wintering rosette starting to sprout in early April in a woodland glade, East Sussex.

Cabbage family

Brassicaceae

Hedge-mustard

Sisymbrium officinale

The hedge-mustard is one of the most common plants of Britain's hedgerows, roadsides, waste-places and arable fields, and, by high summer, it is also usually one of the scruffiest. In size and leaf shape, it is very variable, but, once the capsules start to form, most plants develop a reddish-purple colouration.

Although the leaves often have rather coarse hairs, if you pick them in the spring they can be quite tender. They have a pleasant, slightly peppery flavour, albeit sometimes with a somewhat bitter aftertaste. In some plants this bitterness is strong enough to make the leaves completely inedible.

More consistently palatable are the tops of the young flowering shoots; we highly recommend these as an ingredient for salads.

Left: small plants of hedge mustard.
Right: capsules of hedge mustard pressed to stem, (distinctive feature of this species).
Opposite page: a hedge mustard plant with unusually large, tender, hairless leaves, but with an acutely unpleasant after-taste. Early May, East Sussex.

The sweet violet wth a mass of flowers and new leaves already by early March. Near Hailsham, East Sussex.

Violet Family

Violaceae

The leaves and flowers of all members of the violet family seem to be edible. We have tried most of the British species and find the leaves and flowers to be very good eating and the leaves are often available right through the winter. The roots and the seeds, however, should not be eaten.

Sweet Violet

Viola odorata

This is a very attractive plant, with large round leaves and deep-purple flowers, found by woodland paths and in hedgerows. The big leaves make it very easy to gather a good crop. The one risk is that the largest leaves can be confused with those of winter heliotrope. If you're searching in a place where heliotrope could also be growing, therefore, it would be prudent to look out for the flowers, so you know for sure that you're picking violets.

Marsh Violet
V. palustris

This plant's large, almost hairless leaves make very good eating. It grows in fens, bogs and marshes and on wet heaths, and is often found alongside other edible greens such as the wood stitchwort and the golden saxifrage. The flowers are generally a lilac colour, with darker veins. Marsh violets are found throughout the British Isles, particularly in Scotland, Wales and western Ireland.

Common Dog-violet
V. riviniana

This occurs very commonly throughout the British Isles and is a useful source of greens in very early spring even before the bluish-violet flowers appear. The leaves are tender and have a pleasant mild flavour with a very slight bitterness. The flowers are edible too, but the seeds and roots must be avoided.

The remaining species of violet have leaves and flowers of similar palatability, and can be used as a salad ingredient or as a spinach. The least palatable is the hairy violet (*v.harta*) which is a bit bristly.

Above: marsh violet growing in a boggy glade. Perthshire, late September.

Below: the common ('dog') violet already in flower at the start of April in oak-hazel woodland. East Sussex.

Flowers of bladder-campion.

Chickweed Family

Caryophyllaceae

The leaves of plants of this family are in opposite pairs, rotating at 90 degrees with every successive stem node. The flowers have five sepals joined together into a tube, with protruding points corresponding to the number of component sepals. The petals are red, pink or white. In some cases these five petals are split almost to the base, giving the impression that there are ten. They have either five or ten stamens, an ovary with three to five styles on top, and normally a single hollow inside with a block of tissue in the middle. The many attached ovules are what become the seeds. In all but one case the ovary ripens to a dry capsule, which opens by a number of teeth or valves at the top.

Bladder Campion

Silene vulgaris

This elegant plant can grow to nearly a metre tall, with a mass of stems. The leaves are quite large, normally completely hairless, and have a bloom rather like grapes. The white flowers are about a centimetre and a half wide and each petal is deeply divided down the middle. The plant's name comes from the shape of the sepal tube; it gets inflated so it resembles a bladder.

The shoots, if gathered before the flower starts to form, are succulent, crisp and very palatable, with a mild taste reminiscent of mangetouts and only a very slight bitterness. Some authorities say that the roots are edible, but we've examined them many times and they're always woody, with no sign of anything that could possibly be eaten. The bladder campion is distributed throughout the British Isles, although it's distribution is fairly thin in western Scotland.

Common mouse-ear chickweed (and its close relatives)

Cerastium holosteoides

This hairy little plant has very small pairs of leaves that resemble a mouse's ear. The white flowers are of the usual chickweed type. It is an extremely common plant, found on grassland, dunes, waysides and waste places, as well as on cultivated ground, throughout the British Isles.

Its great merit is that it often survives the winter, so provides a source of winter greens. They're pleasantly crunchy raw, but they become rather stringy if steamed or boiled.

Common mouse-ear chickweed in Perthshire still flowering and producing new shoots in early October.

Water chickweed
Myosoton aquaticum

This resembles the ordinary common chickweed except that it is four times the size. It grows, often very abundantly, on river and stream banks, at lakesides, and in marshes and fens, and is largely limited to the southern part of England. The shoots can reach around 25cm in height and, early in the year, are very pale green, tender and crunchy, with almost no bitterness. At this stage, both leaves and stems are more or less completely hairless, making the shoots very palatable (see photo).

By mid-June, only the top 10cm of the shoots are still good to eat. Although even in late August the newest shoot tips and the leaves further back on the stem are still palatable.

Superficially, the water chickweed looks very similar to the wood chickweed (*Stellaria nemorum*) and the greater chickweed (*Stellaria neglecta*). The water chickweed can be distinguished from both of these partly by its different habitat preference, but also by the fact that whereas the other two have just three styles on the top of their ovary, the water chickweed has five. You can see this quite clearly with the naked eye, although a hand lens will make it even easier to see.

Common chickweed

Stellaria media

This plant has little white flowers and oval, pale-green leaves. The leaves and stalks are generally hairless apart from a very distinctive line of hairs running down one side of the stem. The common chickweed grows in mats low to the ground, and is found throughout the British Isles in arable fields, on waysides and wasteland, and on woodland and marshland fringes.

The youngest, most tender shoots are pleasantly crisp and crunchy. Although they are best eaten raw in salads, they're also good steamed or added to soups and omelettes.

Without its flowers, chickweed can be confused with several other plants. The edible lookalikes include the scarlet pimpernel, which has a square stem, and the yellow pimpernel, which has a round stem which is smooth and hairless.

Common chickweed, showing the diagnostic line of hairs on the stems.

Lesser Stitchwort
Stellaria graminea

This is a smaller version of the greater stitchwort but with far smoother leaves and stems. It grows on wayside verges, on heathland and at woodland edges, and is common and very widespread throughout the whole of Britain. The large white flowers, have petals almost twice the length of the pointed sepals. The leaves are more pointed than those of the bog stitchwort's, especially those on the flowering stalks.

The young vegetative shoots can be harvested throughout the spring and well into the summer, for as long as new ones are being produced, and the plant is so abundant that you can gather a lot in no time at all. The young greens and shoots are excellent chopped up in salads, or lightly boiled or steamed.

Bog Stitchwort
Stellaria uliginosa

This plant thrives not just in bogs but also at the edges of streams, in damp woodland glades and, in the south of England at least, on damp hillsides and meadows. Its young vegetative shoots look similar to those of the lesser stitchwort, except that they're more rounded at the tip, slightly darker green in colour, and above all their flowers have petals shorter than the sepals.

Again, it's the young vegetative shoots that are edible, raw in salads or steamed. Compared to gathering the bigger shoots of the water chickweed, though, gathering the shoot tips of these stitchworts is much more fiddly and less productive.

Opposite page: lesser stitchwort in Perthshire, in flower in mid-September.
Below: bog stitchwort showing the diagnostic feature of the tiny petals being distinctly shorter than the sepals. Boggy forest glade, Perthshire, early October.

Three-nerved chickweed

Three-nerved chickweed.
Harvested young leafy
shoots. early april in
oak-hazel woodland,
Sussex.
Inset: close-up showing
diagnostic veination.

Moehringia trinervia

This plant grows on dry woodland soils throughout almost the entirety of the British Isles, apart from northwest Scotland and most of western Ireland. This plant is distinctly stringier than the common chickweed, so you need to avoid the tougher stems. Raw, they have a very slight bitterness, but steaming largely dispels this and makes them pretty palatable. The name, incidentally, refers to the veination pattern of the leaves.

Sea Sandwort

Honkenya peploides

This remarkable little succulent forms great mats of crunchy green vegetation about three inches thick, and is found right round the coast of Britain, usually on sandy beaches or on shingle beaches with a lot of sand under the surface.

The leafy shoots should be gathered while they're still crisp, turgid and bright green. Once the flowers starts setting seed, the plants get a bit leggy and some of the leaves go flaccid. These succulent shoots are superb in salads.

Above: part of a carpet of sea sandwort on a shingle beach in Sussex, June.

Greater Sea-spurrey

Spergularia media

This little plant grows to about 15cm tall and has long, cylindrical, succulent leaves and whitish or pinkish flowers. It grows very abundantly at the upper edges of mud flats and on sandy sea shores all round the British coast.

The vegetative shoots make an excellent wayside nibble and can also be gathered to add to salads. They have a pleasant 'green' flavour with a slightly alkaline aftertaste, as is so common in maritime plants.

Greater sandspurrey, in mid-August on the Ouse Estuary, East Sussex.

Pigweed is a New World introduction that thrives as a weed of crops such as maize. Its leaves are excellent added to soups and omelets and they make a good spinach. Roasted and ground, the small, black seeds make sustaining dampers.

Goosefoot and samphire family

Chenopodiaceae

This family of plants are mainly herbaceous apart from a few low, slightly woody shrubs. They generally have fleshy or succulent leaves, with a rather mealy, frosted appearance.

The flowers, which form little bunches, are inconspicuous, generally minute and green. Almost all the plants of this family have edible foliage, and many of them also produce easily gatherable seeds.

Fat Hen

Chenopodium album

This is one of the most common weeds of waste places and arable land. Fat hen varies in height from a couple of inches to a metre and a half, and the undersides of the leaves have a distinctive mealy appearance. The raw leaves have a rather strong tangy flavour and most people prefer them cooked as a green vegetable in soups or as a spinach. It produces a mass of flowers and seeds that can be harvested in great quantity. The seeds are ready to be harvested when the knobbly agglomerations of the seeding flowers turn pink (see photo). Stripped dried, rubbed, winnowed, parched and ground into flour, they make very sustaining dampers.

Fat hen forming trusses of tiny flower-buds. For gathering greens, it's already past its best. July, South Downs.

Top left: shoot of fat hen with the flowers at the tips turning pinkish-orange. This is the time to harvest the seed.

Left: fat-hen seeds being stripped into basket.

Bottom left: seeds rubbed out of the enveloping 'sepals' to show their size.

Above: grinding seed of fat hen after drying, rubbing and winnowing. Pershire, late September.

(Photographs: Annette Stickler)

Red goosefoot is a common plant of muck-heaps. Here the plant is in the ideal state for the leaves to be harvested to make spinach or to be added to soups or omeletes. Although the seeds are a lot smaller than those of fat hen, dried, rubbed, winnowed, parched and ground to flour, they make excellent dampers.

Part of a shoot of all-seed (Chenopodium polyspermum) in East Sussex. Like most of the goosefoots the leaves can be used in omelettes and as spinach, and the seeds can be dried, rubbed, winnowed, roasted and ground to make dampers. (The seed-coats are too thick and impervious to be made edible simply by boiling them, as we do with its close relative the domestic quinoa.)

Sea Beet

Beta vulgaris subsp maritima

In the bleak midwinter when you are craving fresh greens, you can't do any better than to go to the shoreline and gather the small leaves produced by the sea beet. It is a rare winter that is so severe as to wipe out these leaves completely. Sea beet grows all round the shores of England and Wales and most of Ireland, but very sparsely in Scotland. It is especially abundant round the south coast of England and grows in great profusion at the high-tide mark of estuarine mud flats, on chalk cliffs and on sand dunes.

Although the plant produces leaves through the winter, they are at their best from late spring to early autumn, when they are much larger. They're better cooked, as they have a rather alkaline taste when raw.

The roots as food

Eaten raw, the roots have a rather bitter aftertaste. Cooked, they are very flavoursome and resemble sweet potatoes; not really surprising as they are the source of the domestic sugar beet.

Top: the knobbly flowers of the sea beet in mid-September.
Above: harvested roots (and leaves) of the sea beet. The roots are relatively thin. Late March.

Above: gathering tender shoots of sea purslane.

Below: sea purslane at Cuckmere estuary.

Sea Purslane

Halimione portulacoides

The grey leaves of this low shrub dominate the mud flats along the coasts of England, Wales and eastern Ireland, although it is almost absent from Scotland.

Purslane shoots and leaves are very palatable, and are available and edible year-round. The green shoots make a perfect wayside nibble, or you can gather them in greater quantity to take home and steam. The youngest and most tender shoots are those formed in spring and early summer, but the older shoots can still be used at other times of the year. In the winter plants growing above the high-tide point are less prone to frost damage. And their leaves, that remain grey-green rather than turning yellow, these are finer the most suitable as food.

Annual Seablite

Suaeda maritima

This plant grows to about a foot tall, and has fleshy cylindrical leaves, usually with a reddish tinge. They often grow in great numbers just below the high-tide mark. The young shoots are tender, crisp and succulent, and make an excellent wayside nibble, although they're also good steamed. The annual seablite grows in salt marshes and on sea shores all round the coast of Britain.

Crisply succulent plants of annual sea blight in late July, with flower-buds forming and ready for harvesting Cuckmere Estuary, East Sussex.

Marsh samphire, or glasswort

Salicornia (various species)

This is one of the few wild plants that is sold commercially in the British Isles.

The plants grow between 6 and 8 inches, and their glistening, succulent green stems cover the lower stretches of tidal mud flats. Traditionally they would have been uprooted, but as this is now illegal you have to cut them with a pair of scissors or a blade. Marsh samphire can be eaten raw as a delicious wayside nibble, steamed or even pickled.

A new crop of young plants of marsh samphire on tidal mud-flats. Late August, Ouse estuary, East Sussex.

171

Mallow family

Malvacaea

Common mallow

The common mallow (*Malva sylvestris*) has large clumps of round leaves on long stalks with radial veins. The flowers measure about 4cm across and are truly remarkable, with purplish-mauve petals, cerise-red stamens and filaments fused into a tube and creamy-coloured pollen-producing anthers. The brightly coloured styles bear off the stigmatic surfaces to receive pollen from other flowers.

The leaves can be made into a sort of spinach, although it is rather glutinous. Because of the leaves' mucilaginousness, they make a very good soup. You can also eat the immature fruiting structure, traditionally known as 'cheeses', which consists of a disc of tissue with radially-arranged compartments, each containing a single seed. All mallow species produce these delicacies, with the exception of the musk mallow, which has very long hairs that make the fruiting structure unpalatable.

Some of the literature suggests eating the roots of the common mallow and those of its near neighbour the dwarf mallow. We have found old ones so woody that there is no possibility of eating them.

The flowers can be added to salads.

Left: marsh mallow in flower on Pevensey Marshes.

Middle: roots of young plant.

Right: mallow 'cheeses' – the immature green fruits. make an excellent wayside nibble. (On the plant these discs eventually split into one-seeded units.)

Marsh Mallow

Althaea officinalis

Today the confections we call marshmallows are made of starch, gelatine, sugar and dyes, but in the past the raw materials were provided by the roots of this elegant plant. Its green stems stand about a metre tall, with ranks of soft, velvety grey-green leaves and pale pink, dark-centred flowers about 3cm across or more. Marsh mallow grows in some profusion in coastal marshes, mainly in the southern half of England and Wales and in southwest Ireland.

Marsh mallow has a huge root system, with intertwined masses of young roots. The heavy clay soil that the plants seem to favour and the interlocked roots of other plants, such as meadowsweet, would have made digging out the entire root system extremely hard work, if not almost impossible. However, the smaller younger roots growing around the outside of the root mass are starch-rich, crunchy and very palatable raw or steamed, with a sweet flavour and they could have been harvested without digging up the entire root mass.

The roots are edible right through the winter, and could have been found easily thanks to the tough, bleached remains of the flower-bearing stalks. These persist through the winter and well into the following spring even in the most exposed, windblown locations.

Geranium Family

Geraniaceae

Common Storksbill

Erodium cicutarium

This plant thrives on dunes, dry grassland and arable fields, and particularly favours sandy soils. It occurs across most of the British Isles, especially around the coast. It is typically about calf-high with finely-divided leaves and small, pink flowers. It superficially resembles herb robert (*Geranium robertianum*). The key difference between the two, though, is that the leaves of the storksbill are very palatable, while those of the herb robert have a rather peculiar flavour. Storksbill leaves have a mild nutty flavour with a very slightly bitter aftertaste and are good for salads. They're also very pleasant lightly steamed.

It's easy enough to distinguish storksbill from herb robert. Storksbill plants have leaves that divide into leaflets arranged in two ranks, one either side of the midrib or rachis of the leaf apinnace arrangement, whereas herb robert has leaves that are palmately divided, which is to say that the segments and their stalks radiate out from a central point.

Typical leaf-rosette of a common storksbill growing on sandy soil near Blackmore, Hants, September.

Wood Sorrel

Oxalis acetosella

Wood sorrel seldom grows much more than 10cm tall and each of its leaves has three heart-shaped leaflets rather like a clover. The difference is that, whereas in the clover the stalks of the leaves come in on the same plane as these three leaflets, in the wood sorrel the stalk comes in at 90 degrees to the three leaflets. Also, the leaflets have a tendency to fold down when it's raining, and at night. The flowers emerge tightly furled and open up into a 2cm-wide bell of five white petals.

The leaves are the only edible part and need to be stripped from the thin, wiry stalks. They taste deliciously sour and lemony, and make an excellent addition to salads. They're also a very good stuffing for fish. However, the leaves contains free oxalic acid, so wood-sorrel leaves should be eaten in moderation.

The large buds on the plant's creeping rhizomes are also very sour, so presumably they contain oxalic acid too and should be treated with caution.

At a depth of between 15 and 20cm, attached to the rhizome network, are small tap roots about 5 or 6cm long and 8 or 9mm wide, with a glossy, semi-transparent look. They are sweet and sugary and also quite numerous, making them a potentially significant food resource.

Top: wood sorrel flowers. May, Sussex.
Bottom: leaves gathered from dense sward of wood sorrell in spruce woodland, Perthshire, late October.

Pea family

Fabaceae

With 600 genera and 13,000 species worldwide, this family ranks as the world's third biggest plant family after thistle and dandelion families, and the orchid family.

The pea family has a number of very distinctive features. Firstly, the flowers, rather than being radially symmetrical like the buttercup and dog rose, are bilaterally symmetrical. They have a large standard petal at the back of the flower, two small wing petals at the side, and a pair of narrower petals that fuse together at their lower edge to form a 'keel' protecting the carpels and stamens. Secondly the ovary consists of just one ovary, in the form of a legume, which sheds its seeds at maturity by splitting down two sutures. Thirdly nine out of ten, or sometimes all ten, of the filaments of the stamens are fused together to form a tube that surrounds the young legume in flower. The fourth distinguishing feature is that all nutrient storage is in the seed leaves of the embryo (the cotlyedons).

The most important and frequently available foodstuff from this plant family are the seeds. However, it is crucial to remember that the seeds of most legumes are safe to eat only when they are young, green and tender and gathered from young green pods, as most of them develop toxins as they reach maturity. Even in their young state, though, they shouldn't be eaten in huge quantities, some of tem contain potentially hazardous compounds even at this stage. Vetches and vetchlings are so widely available and abundant that we speculate that they would have been used for food by our Mesolithic ancestors.

Gathering the tangled vines of tufted vetch, complete with their green pods, in late July.

Above right: the small but succulent green seeds.

Opposite page top left: tender young shoots of the common vetch emerging in late March on the Sussex coast.
Top right: young shoots gathered for a salad.
Left: shoot with green pods.

Common vetch

Vicia sativa

This annual is easily distinguished from its close relative, the bush vetch, by its rich purplish-crimson flowers, the calyx teeth that are as long as the calyx tube, and by the black patch on many of its half-arrowhead-shaped stipules. It occurs throughout the British Isles, but is most common in the south of England where it grows in great profusion in hedges and road verges, and in grassy places in general.

By late March or early April the end six to eight centimeters of the shoots can be plucked and eaten raw or steamed. You shouldn't eat too many on their own, but they are perfectly safe as one component of a salad. Later in the year, you need to gather only the very tip of the shoots.

The green seedpods are available later in the year in some quantity and for quite a long period. The fresh young seeds make a perfect wayside snack.

The bush vetch, like the other legumes, ensuring the continuous supply of edible green seeds by the vines continuing to grow and form new flowers throughout the summer.

Bush Vetch

Vicia sepium

This perennial's flowers are purple, the leaves are elliptical in shape, and the lower calyx teeth are much shorter than the calyx tube. It grows in hedges, thickets and other grassy places, and is very common throughout the British Isles. The young shoots can be eaten as described for the common vetch, although as they are slightly stringier you should choose shoots that are chunkier and that snap off easily.

The seeds are very similar in abundance and flavour to those of the common vetch, so could have served as a significant food resource.

Tufted Vetch

Vicia cracca

This is largely a hedgerow plant and is abundant throughout Britain. It has masses of rich blue-purple flowers, crowded into racemes. The pods that form from the flowers are not very big and the seeds are a little smaller than the first two vetches discussed, so gathering them is quite a fiddly job. Also, the leafy shoots of this species tend to be rather stringy, and so we rarely use them.

Above right: tufted vetch, Etchingham, Sussex. Late July.

181

Hairy Tare
Vicia hirsuta

Tares are a much more delicate version of vetches. Their trailing stems are more slender, their leaves are only about half the size of the leaves of the other vetches, and the pods, which are rarely much longer than 15mm, contain just four seeds. The inconspicuous flowers are a pale whitish-purple. Although, the shoot tips are a bit stringy they can be steamed, but they're not very substantial. The seeds are small. Hairy tare occurs throughout the British Isles but is concentrated in the more southerly parts of England.

Other vetches
Vicia spp.

There are several other vetches native to Britain that could be used for food in the way discussed above. These include the wood vetch (*V. sylvatica*), the yellow vetch (*V. lutea*), the spring vetch (*V. lathyroides*) and finally the bithynian vetch (*V. bithynica*). We can also perhaps include additional tares here, particularly the smooth tare (*V. tetrasperma*).

Below left: vines of hairy tare with flowers and green pods. East Sussex.
Below right: the green pods.
Bottom right: some of the green pods and their seeds stripped from the vines. Perthshire, late September.

The Native Everlasting Pea

Lathyrus sylvestris

This is a spectacular plant and very large, with broadly winged stems, big leaflets and lots of tendrils. The flowers are almost 2cm long and rose-pink, and produce pods almost the size of narrow pea pods. The plant is found in hedgerows, thickets and woodland glades and on woodland margins. It is scattered across southern England and parts of Wales, and in a few locations in southern Scotland.

Although the pods are almost the size of pea pods, their pod walls are very rough from the outset and there's no pause in their growth while they tendril up, so they can't be eaten as mangetouts. However, the pods produce ten or more seeds of roughly the size of small peas; 8 to 9mm across in many cases. They grow in great abundance and, eaten fresh and raw, taste just like very fresh garden peas. It seems highly likely that our Mesolithic forebears would have made ample use of this rich resource.

Above: the prolific everlasting pea in hedgerows near Bignor, West Sussex.

Above left: meadow vetchling with green pods ready to harvest. East Sussex. Above right: the green seeds a welcome wayside nibble.

Meadow Vetchling

Lathyrus pratensis

This is one of our most common vetchlings and is found in hedges, waysides and verges and other grassy places. It grows throughout the British Isles apart from the northernmost Scottish Highlands. It produces flowers for five or more months of the year, but not in great numbers. The number of pods per plant is therefore not that huge, but nevertheless they are well worth gathering. The seeds are small, about the same size as those of the tufted vetch, alongside which it often grows.

Bitter Vetch

Lathyrus linifolius

The bitter vetch is native British and produces edible tubers, although large-scale consumption of them is really only for liquorice fanatics.

The bitter vetch occurs throughout the British Isles apart from in the southeast Midlands and East Anglia and central Ireland. It grows among grassy vegetation in forest glades, woodland fringes, thickets and hedge banks. The flowers start out as a crimson colour but soon turn blue-purple and then dull blue or green. The seeds are really too small to bother with. The tubers grow about 10cm below the surface and are a dark chocolate-brown in colour and about 3cm across. On any one plant there might be three or four conjoined tubers. The flesh is pure white, crunchy and hard, but it becomes slightly softer when steamed, boiled or roasted. The tubers have an extremely strong, sweet liquorice flavour with a slight bitter aftertaste.

Above: a pair of tubers from just part of a plant.
Below: flowering shoots of the bitter vetch in early June, Sussex Weald.

185

Pea family

Fabaceae

White clover

Trifolium repens

Clover heads, with their 40 or so little florets, develop to a correspondingly large number of little pods that, while still green and tender, can be eaten in their entirety: pods, seeds, and all. It's also easy to gather them in bulk; simply strip the clover heads complete with their dead brown floret remains. They can then be dried and ground to a flour.

You need to catch the plants when the seeds are as replete as possible with storage carbohydrates and other nutrients, but before they become dangerous to eat. You have to be doubly careful as ripening happens in stages from the top to the bottom of each head. There are four markers that we use to determine ripeness and edibility. Firstly, all the petals of all the florets have to be completely brown; secondly, the sepal tubes have lost their patches of very pale green and are more uniformly green or have turned brown; thirdly, the reflexed pedicels (visible at the top of the head), which were previously pale green, are again more solidly green or have turned brown (the pedicels are the stalks of the individual florets); fourthly, the peduncles (that's the stalk to the head as a whole) are still green or beginning to turn yellow but have not yet turned brown. This last marker is extremely important. See the photographs for further clarification.

Dampers made from these dried and ground up heads have a slightly dry texture but almost no bitterness, and a definite sweetness, and are very sustaining.

Because the white clover is so abundant, it seems entirely possible that its pods were used as food by our Mesolithic forebears, although we have no evidence from the archaeology so far.

Young shoots

These can be gathered in early spring, certainly before the middle of April. They are not very inspiring.

Top: a sea of white clover on the downs above Glyndebourne, East Sussex
Bottom left: a single head of florets.
Middle: a clump of freshly-emerged leafy shoots of white clover, in early April on the Sussex coast.
Middle right: a fruiting head of white clover with the tips of the tiny green pods protruding from the florets.
Middle bottom: the tiny green pods excised from the head so you can see what they look like. Most of them have seeds.
Bottom right: gathering fruiting heads in late September at the optimal state of maturity. Perthshire.

Red clover in early
August, East Sussex.

Red Clover

Trifolium pratense

Red-clover seeds can be gathered in much the same way as those of the white clover. The big difference, though, is that red clover pods don't look like miniature pea pods; instead, they're roundish structures with a single seed inside, quite a bit larger than the seeds of the white clover. The young shoot can also be picked and eaten in the same way, but they make equally uninspiring eating.

Other large-headed clovers that can be gathered and used in the same way include the zig-zag clover (*T. medium*) and the strawberry clover (*T. fragiferum*).

The rose family

Rosaceae

The rose family encompasses a huge array of plants with edible fruits, ranging from apples to cherries, rose hips to plums, and haws to strawberries. Some of them are so spectacularly different from each other that, at first sight, it seems inconceivable that they belong to the same family. Indeed, some taxonomists (taxonomy is the science of classification) have suggested that the rose family should be split into at least two separate families.

Nevertheless, members of this family do all have a number of basic features in common. For example, most of the flowers have five sepals, five free (unjoined) petals, and lots of free stamens (generally two to four times the number of sepals). The internal anatomy of their seeds shares even more fundamental features. They also have a number of chemical criteria in common. For example, they protect their fruits and seeds (particularly the kernels of their fruit stones) by lacing them with compounds called cyanogenic glycosides that release cyanide as soon as any cells are damaged, for example by hapless herbivores eating the fruits.

Although most of the trees of this family seldom grow to a great size, in ancient woodland trees such as the wild cherry can tower to 25m and develop massive trunks. But even the family members that grow only as shrubs or small trees provide important components of lowland woodland, as they doubtless did in Mesolithic Britain. In fact in some areas of Britain the family commonly contributes a quarter or more of the total woodland cover. And spiny family members like the hawthorns, blackthorns, bullaces, wild roses and brambles still dominate lowland hedgerows, where their spines are invaluable for helping to confine livestock. Closer to the highland zone, it is more often the rowan, bird cherry and wild raspberry, along with the omnipresent bramble (blackberry), that grow in particular abundance.

The raspberry group includes raspberries, blackberries, dewberries and cloudberries. All of these fruits are agglomerations of 'drupelets' attached to a conical, white, pithy core (the 'receptacle'). The individual drupelets are miniaturized replicas of stone fruits ('drupes') such as plums and cherries. Each consists of a tiny stone with an even tinier seed inside, a juicy layer of flesh, and a thin skin. In raspberries, the conjoined drupelets become detached from the receptacle when they're picked, leaving the receptacle on the stem. Being able to eat the drupelets without the fibrous receptacle is what gives raspberries their delicious softness.

Wild raspberries growing in woodland on the South Downs, Hampshire.

Raspberry

Rubus idaeus

The raspberry grows throughout most of Britain, although it is nothing like as abundant as the common bramble. Its delicious, soft red fruits, which come away from the pithy core when picked, are very distinctive, as are the woody shoots ('canes'). Unlike bramble, with its sombre-coloured leaves, vicious, hooked spines, and purplish stems that loop over and root at the tip, raspberry canes grow tall and erect with yellowish bark, are modestly armed with slender, straight prickles, and have bright green leaves with, typically, a white, felted underside. Raspberry canes are biennial: new ones grow from the rootstock in the latter half of the year, flower and fruit the following summer, then die back completely, to be replaced by a new cane.

Wild raspberries are relatively rare in areas with dry soils, and the fruits can be gathered in quantity only in well-watered habitats. Scotland, with its ample rainfall, is rightly famed for productive wild populations, as well as being a world leader in commercial raspberry production.

Raspberries must surely be among the most delicious of all wild fruits, with their soft texture and effervescent combination of sweetness and tartness. Our Mesolithic ancestors doubtless feasted on fresh raspberries wherever they were available, and records of recent hunter-gatherers suggest that they probably stored them over the winter. Certainly, records suggest that this was standard practice among many of the indigenous peoples of North America. Some groups dried the fruits, like raisins. The Woods Cree preserved them, dried, together with fish or in fish oil. The Okanagan-Colville crushed them to make juice as did the Micmac. The Fisherman-Lake Slave "boiled them and placed them in birch-bark baskets in the sun to dry, then stored the dried loaves in a cache, to be broken into pieces and boiled before being eaten" (Kuhnlein and Turner 1991). The climate in Mesolithic Britain was doubtless too damp to dry thick raspberry loaves, but mushed or boiled raspberries could probably have been dried in thin sheets as fruit leather.

Monkton, an archaebotanist reconstructing the diet of the ancient Huron Indians, has calculated that, despite the Huron cultivating maize as their principal caloric staple, raspberries and other soft fruit probably met as much as a quarter of their annual caloric need, as well as supplying valuable nutrients including provitamin A, vitamins B1, B2 and C, and minerals such as calcium, iron, potassium, phosphorus and copper.

Raspberry pips turn up on archaeological sites in the British Isles from all periods. In most cases they have been preserved in deposits unconnected with human consumption, but their very presence proves that raspberries were locally available. Having said that, the remains of mediaeval cesspits, sewers, latrines and garderobes are occasionally found, and their faecal remains commonly include of raspberry pips.

Top: blackberries gathered for immediate use. We have found that traditional (pre-freezer) methods of preserving soft fruit leave blackberries tasting insipid.
Above: spring harvest of crisp shoot-tips of bramble. They are excellent steamed or blended into nettle soup. Always use thick shoot-tips that snap off crisply and whose spines are still soft and not the thin wiry ones.

Blackberry (bramble)

The Rubus fruticosus aggregate

The range of forms of the blackberry is huge: a botanist called WCR Watson, in his *Handbook of the Rubi of Great Britain and Ireland*, describes some 286 species. Because they are very similar to each other they are known as 'micro-species' and grouped together as the 'Rubus fruticosus aggregate'.

The berries grow in clusters at the end of the shoots, which die after two or three years of cropping. In his *Food for Free*, Richard Mabey explains that the "berry right at the tip of the stalk – is the first to ripen and is the sweetest and fattest of all. Eat it raw. A few weeks later, the other berries near the end ripen; these are less juicy, but are still good for jams and pies. The small berries further back on the stalk do not ripen until October. They are hard and slightly bitter, and are only really useful if cooked with other fruit." The autumn pudding, in which blackberries are combined with other autumn fruits such as bullaces, sloes, elderberries and crab-apples, is a delicious way to use the more bitter berries.

Interestingly, we have found that traditional methods of preserving soft fruit leave blackberries tasting insipid.

The crisp shoot-tips are also edible and are excellent steamed, or blended into a nettle soup, although you should always be careful to choose thick tips that snap off crisply and whose spines are still soft.

Blackberry pips are perhaps the most commonly found wild-food plant seeds on archaeological sites in Britain. The finds follow a pattern similar to that found in raspberries (see above).

One of the myriad forms of blackberry.

Dewberry

Rubus caesius

Dewberries typically differ from blackberries in having just a few, large, juicy drupelets in each fruit. The drupelets have a conspicuous waxy bloom that makes them appear bluish. Once ripe, they can often be easily detached from the receptacle. The stems are much weaker and the spines much more poorly developed than in most blackberries. Archaeological finds follow the same pattern as those of raspberries.

Cloudberry

Rubus chamaemorus

Up on the bleak, high moorlands of Scotland and northern England there are few instantly edible plant foods. This makes the tasty cloudberry a plant to be cherished, especially in patches where it produces good yields. Most British populations, however, produce only small fruits, and these only sporadically. Of course, the bleak moorlands of the present day, heavily grazed and severely deforested, are a very different landscape to that of the Mesolithic, when the mountains would have been cloaked in woodland and carried a much broader range of wild foods.

However, in the northern tundra, cloudberry bushes still produce vast yields. Indeed, from the ethnographic literature it is clear that, among the indigenous peoples of northernmost Europe, Asia, Alaska and Canada, cloudberries were a staple food, often second only to bilberries, and were particularly prized as they were among the first to ripen.

Cloudberries were also commonly stored for the winter. Pierpoint Johnson (1862) reports that "The Laplanders bury them in the snow, and thus preserve them through the long arctic winter, until the season when such acid fruits are peculiarly wholesome and acceptable." Kuhnlein & Turner (1991) further describe the Haida and Tsimshian picking cloudberries "in mid-summer, when they were still hard, and storing them under water and grease in bentwood cedar boxes .... Sometimes they were scalded briefly before being stored."

The cloudberry plant is small, at just 5-20cm tall, and bears berries with relatively few, largish drupelets that are initially scarlet, but ripen to a shade of yellow or salmon-pink.

The cloudberry is a mere 5-20cm tall and bears a single berry with relatively few, largish drupelets that are initiallly scarlet, but ripen to a shade of yellow or salmon-pink.

195

Silverweed

Potentilla anserine

To appreciate the softness of silverweed's tufts of silky-sheened leaves you have to feel them. It's no wonder they used to be used to line the boots of weary ploughmen and footsore soldiers! For our forager ancestors, however, the silver-green tufts would also have provided easily-spotted markers for what is the most nutrient-rich and palatable of our indigenous root-foods.

Silverweed grows throughout the British Isles but can form particularly dense swards in areas like river terraces, which are flooded in winter, and in coastal marshes on stabilized areas above the mud-flats.

In addition to its normal, fibrous roots, each mature plant produces between one and six storage roots. These range from straw-coloured to nearly black, and are generally rather scrawny: a mere 3-7mm in diameter, roughly parallel-sided, and 15 to 30cm long. However, under the thin skin of these unpromising-looking roots is gleaming white, crisp-textured storage tissue, very edible and packed with starch.* The roots are extremely brittle, with no stringiness, and the crunchy texture, combined with their nutty flavour, makes them absolutely delicious to eat raw. They are however much more digestible when cooked, whether by steaming, light roasting, or dried, ground to flour and made into dampers. Whichever way, they have a starchy texture and are very sustaining.

We were not surprised, therefore, when nutrient analyses revealed exceptionally high concentrations of assimilable starch: 31g per 100g of fresh root. This is significantly higher than the content of cultivated potatoes and, together with burdock root, is the highest starch concentration of any root food we've analysed so far.

In nineteenth-century Scotland the folklorist Alexander Carmichael noted that silverweed roots continued to be both cultivated and gathered from the wild until the arrival of the potato. Indeed, he records that it was claimed on North Uist that "A man could sustain himself on silverweed from a square of ground his own length." Although this seems a little over-optimistic, there are eighteenth-century records from Perthshire of people using silverweed roots as one of just two caloric staples (the other being the pignut).

The roots also served as a staple for at least 20 different indigenous hunter-gatherer peoples in northwestern North America. They were generally eaten after several hours of steaming, or sometimes baked in hot ashes. Roots were also gathered especially for storage over the winter, for which purpose they were normally steamed and dried.

In Central Asia, too, silverweed dominated diet wherever the supplies were sufficient. Also, in his remarkable *Geschichte unserer Pflanzennahrung*, Maurizio (1927) describes the roots as the 'favourite food of the Tanguts' – a people of North Eastern Tibet. Similar examples of silverweed dependence come from the Tarim Basin in Zinjiang (West China) and from Yakutia (now the Sar Republic) in the Russian Far East (eastern Turkmenistan).

The best time to gather the roots is in early autumn, as soon as the leaves start to turn orange or brown, although they continue to offer good eating through the winter and into the spring. Above-ground markers are called for, though, as the leaves die off and decompose fairly early.

In the spring, tender new roots, white and often mauve- or purple-tinged, grow out of the central stock. During the summer, these new roots slowly start to fill with starch and other nutrients, turn a yellowish-brown, and are eventually fit for eating again.

Although the roots do not grow down very deep, digging them up is very hard work, especially on the heavy, sticky clay soils that the plants so often favour. It always requires a spade, mattock or digging stick. However, the effort expended in digging seems to be more than compensated for by the fact that no processing is needed.

So far we know of no remains of silverweed roots on archaeological sites, but there is evidence that they were very widespread in prehistory. It seems highly likely to us that silverweed played a major role in the diet of the hunter-gatherers of Mesolithic Britain. The roots are extremely palatable; they're packed with energy; the plants are common throughout most of the British Isles; they often grow densely and prolifically; the roots do not grow too deep so are not overly difficult to dig up they require minimal processing; cooking is straight-forward; they can also be eaten raw; and once dried, they can be stored for long periods.

Wild strawberries in woodland
on South Downs, near Bignor,
East Sussex.

Rose Family

Rosaceae

Wild Strawberry
Fragaria vesca

Wild strawberries are the first fruit of the year to ripen, usually appearing in early June, and the plants usually continue to produce fruit until the end of August or even later. They are widespread throughout the British Isles, with the exception of the most northerly areas of Scotland. They are to be found in shady woodland glades and on grassy banks.

The fruit are delicious raw, but in large enough quantities they are also superb in dishes like summer pudding. If there is no fruit present, you can tell whether you're looking at the wild strawberry or the barren strawberry (*Potentilla sterilis*), by the leaves; those of the barren strawberry are a much darker green, the hairs on the underside of the leaf stick out where the wild strawberry's leaf hairs are flattened, and the terminal tooth of the barren strawberry's leaf is shorter than those on either side of it, whereas in the true wild strawberry the tooth is as long as or longer than the rest. The young leaves both the wild strawberry and the barren strawberry can be eaten in salads.

Parsley Pierts

Aphanes arvensis and A. microcarpa

Lesser parsley piert seldom grows taller than 5cm, and even the larger species, *arvensis*, rarely exceeds 10cm. Parsley piert is widely distributed throughout most of Britain, mainly in sandy soils. Traditionally it was used as a pickle as well as being eaten raw.

Above left: the diminutive parsley piert in late September, with match as scale. Perthshire.
Above right: part of an extensive sward of the even tinier lesser parsley piert in late May on dry, sandy soil in the Sussex High Weald.

Salad Burnet

Poterium sanguisorba

This plant has a mass of tiny purple, crimson and mauve flowers, on stalks no taller than 30cm. Salad burnet is most common in southern England, particularly on chalk downs. The tiny rosettes are distinctly off-putting both to touch and to taste, but the salad burnet does actually come into its own in well watered, lightly grazed environments. The plant in the photograph, with its lovely soft foliage, was found growing beside a stream in the Chilterns in just such a micro-habitat. Obviously, then, it's best to target this kind of environment if you're looking for salad burnet leaves to eat.

The younger leaves are good chopped up in salad and the coarser ones can be steamed.

The great burnet (*Sanguisorba officinalis*) grows to a metre tall and has a much bigger rosette of leaves and flowering heads, usually a deep maroon colour. In moist conditions it can be very abundant. The leaves can be used in just the same way as those of the salad burnet, although they can be distinctly bitter. Great burnet is most common from Oxford up through the Midlands to the Lake District.

Above: salad burnet growing on stream bank in the Chilterns in early September.
Right: a flowering head, with its pink-red stigmas and purple-stalked stamens.

The dog rose and its relatives

Rosa canina, etc.

Dog rose and its relatives grow mostly in hedgerows and have pink-tinged flowers. The shiny red rosehips are remarkable, not just for their huge range of shapes and sizes, but also for their uniquely high concentration of vitamin C. With levels of up to 2000mg per 100g of fruit, they have the highest concentration of this nutrient of any wild fruit in Britain. This was recognised in the Second World War, when there was widespread fear that the lack of imported fruit would result in vitamin-C deficiency in the British population. The Ministry of Health organised the collection of wild rosehips by volunteers on a truly massive scale, and issued very precise directions on how to prepare rosehip syrup with minimal loss of the precious vitamin C. It is interesting to note that there was clearly awarenessthat vitamin C is likely to be lost – not from being briefly boiled (a common fallacy, even today) but from the hip-flesh being crushed. The instructions make certain that is avoided by promptly immersing the freshly crushed hips in boiling water. The directions were so meticulous that we feel we must present them here in full:

"Have ready 3 pints (1.5 litres) of boiling water, mince the hips in a coarse mincer, copy immediately into the boiling water or if possible mince the hips directly into the boiling water and again bring to the boil. Stop heating and put aside for 15 minutes. Pour into a flannel or linen crash jelly bag and allow to drip until the bulk of the liquid has come through. Return the residue to the saucepan, add 1½ pints of boiling water, stir and allow to stand for 10 minutes. Pour back into the jelly bag and allow to drip. To make sure all the sharp hairs are removed, put back the first half cupful of liquid and allow to drip through again. Put the mixed juice into a clean saucepan and boil down until the juice measures about 1½ pints, then add 1¾ lb of sugar and boil for a further 5 minutes. Pour into hot sterile bottles and seal at once. If corks are used, these should have been boiled for ¼ hour just previously and after insertion coated with melted paraffin wax. It is advisable to use small bottles and the syrup will not keep for more than a week or two once the bottle is opened. Store in a dark cupboard." (From *Hedgerow Harvest*, Ministry of Food, 1943).

It is important to add that, although the flesh of the fruit makes good eating, you must rinse the seeds and hairs away thoroughly as they can cause choking and serious irritation of the throat.

In addition to the vitamin C, rosehips contain an impressive array of other nutrients, particularly pro-vitamin A, vitamins of the B group, vitamins P and K and vitamin E. They can also contain up to 12 per cent sugars. As rosehips occur so widely and prolifically in Britain, and remain available well into the winter, we consider them to be a hugely important and useful survival food.

You can stew the hips to make a mush, which is good either as a fruit dish on its own or as an accompaniment to other foods. Alternatively the fruits can be made into rosehip tea – and rather than throwing away the solid matter at the bottom of your cup you can eat it as a tasty and nutritious extra.

Top: rosehips split open to show the seeds interspersed with bristly hairs.
Middle: identifying wild roses to species can be problematic. New Forest, Hampshire.
Above: tender young rose shoots that snap off crisply are excellent steamed. Ardeche Gorge (France), early May.

The distinctive black hip of the burnet rose. Early September, Sussex coast.

Burnet Rose

Rosa pimpinellifolia

The burnet rose is a creeping deciduous shrub that can grow up to a metre high. However, on sand dunes and on shingle beaches it tends to grow low to the ground, reaching only about 30cm high but covering quite an area. The stems are smothered in straight spines and fine bristles and the flowers are normally quite large and an ivory-white colour. But the most distinctive feature of the burnet rose are its hips, which are shiny and black with a crown of upward-pointing sepals. The burnet rose occurs widely all over the British Isles, particularly in coastal areas.

Japanese Rose

Rosa rugosa

Although this is a native of northern China, Korea and Japan, we include it here because it often occurs in Britain as an escapee from cultivation and sometimes reverts to its wild form. It is instantly recognisable by its large, pink or mauve, crumpled-looking petals. The hips are huge, much wider than they are long, and the stems positively bristle with spines.

The other reason for including this rose is that it has very high concentrations of vitamin C, not to mention high levels of other antioxidants and nutrients including keratin, flavonoids, B-group vitamins, and vitamins P and K. Its hips are quicker to process than the hips of the other roses as they soften very quickly and are therefore very easy to turn into a mush.

Above: naturalised Japanese rose in late August on the Sussex coast.
Below: some of the hips already going soft.

Stone-Fruit Tribe

This tribe includes the sloe, bullace, plum, cherry and cherry laurel.

Our ancestors may have used and preserved members of this tribe by drying and by making them into fruit leathers. There is evidence of dried slices of crab-apple in archaeological records. Slicing the fruit thinly aids desiccation and renders them sweeter and less astringent. Bullace or wild damson, wild grapes, barberries, cherries, whitebeam fruits and sloe berries may well also have been dried.

To make fruit leathers, the fruit is crushed into a paste and spread thinly onto sheets of bark or other material and allowed to dry. This process also cuts down tartness and astringency, plus fruit preserved in this way is much easier to transport than fresh fruit. Heating also frees the sugars in the fruit and makes them sweeter and more palatable.

Blackthorn (sloe)

Prunus spinosa

Blackthorn is one of Britain's most common trees or shrubs. Its prolific suckering and tangles of black, spine-clad branches dominate many hedgerows and woodland fringes. In winter, blackthorn bushes are bare, black and appear to be dead, but by the spring they are smothered with white blossom. They often continue flowering for several weeks, and once flowering is almost over the leaves start to appear.

Each of the plant's vicious, 1-3-inch-long spines has flower and leaf-buds arrayed along its length. Once dead, the spines stay sharp but become very brittle and, if impaled, make sure you excise any spines that are left behind, as such wounds often go septic.

Freshly picked, the flower buds offer a unique wayside snack, and their almond flavour adds something special to a salad. They're at their tastiest when the buds are just bursting, but it's best not to over-indulge: the almond aroma comes from a toxic compound called amygdalin and from the even more toxic hydrogen cyanide (HCN) that amygdalin releases when the flowers are crushed between the teeth. The flowers are also known to have a laxative effect.

Gathering sloes by plucking them from the bush is very inefficient and risks our being impaled by the spines. Beating is a better and safer method.

Large numbers of sloe stones are regularly recovered from archaeological sites in circumstances suggesting that they were eaten. However, although the ethnographic literature regularly mentions their being used to make sloe jelly or to flavour drinks, it rarely says anything about their use as a significant food and says nothing about any procedures followed to make them edible.

Freshly plucked, sloes are completely inedible: due to their malic acid content they are intensely sour, and also mouth-dryingly astringent and often bitter. Heating them has

a sweetening effect and reduces the bitterness, but rarely helps the astringency. Exposing the sloes to frost makes them very sweet, while retaining their delicious tanginess. They still have some astringency though and this can be removed by bruising or crushing the fruits.

Simply bruising them by, for example, rolling them between flat slabs of rock, is too slow for the purposes of bulk processing. Crushing the fruit into a mash is quicker, and eliminates the astringency while again retaining a zingy tartness. This mash can be eaten in considerable quantities as a seasonal staple.

If the mash is to be stored, or if it's too sour, it needs heating. It can be squeezed into small flat cakes and heated to make a thick, textured fruit leather. Heating the cakes is also an effective storage technique as it kills fungal spores and helps seal the surface against attack by spoilage further micro-organisms.

Top left: beware the spines!
Top right: blackthorn in flower in Marden, East Sussex.
Above: unripe sloes in September.

Top: sloes almost ripe in mid-October.

Middle: ripe sloes in early November. A quarter of them were already wrinkled, but we were still awaiting the first frost.

Above: Gordon harvesting by beating sloes into a long-handled basket in mid-November.

Top: sloe harvest – Ray removing twigs.

Above: sieving sloes harvested by beating to remove smaller twigs and stalks.

Top: roasting sloes on fire.

Middle: early December, after the first frost, some sloes wrinkled, but most still smooth (the latter were the sweetest).

Above left: frosted sloes being crushed in a wooden pestle and mortar to initiate elimination of astringency.

Above right: the sloes beng crushed.

Top: you can also use a stone pestle and mortar.

Middle: paste squeezed into cakes and left for two days to allow enzymes to de-activate tannins.

Above: after two days of 'curing' the crushed sloe cakes are ready for light roasting.

Traditional grafting onto wild trees of the rose family in south east Turkey. All the scattered trees are wild species of pear, cherry, plum and almond which seeded themselves spontaneously but onto which local farmers have grafted domestic varieties. Augusta Tunceli Province. We suspect that equivalent practices were applied in the British Isles after the arrival of farming.

Three feral plums

All three of these plums appear to have been introduced into Britain and are found across the British Isles, most commonly in southeastern England, but occasionally as far north as southern Scotland.

All of them include varieties in which the fruits are, or were traditionally, eaten fresh, roasted or stewed, dried into prunes, or turned into fruit leathers. As with cherries, the congealed gums that exude wherever the bark is wounded are reported to be both edible and nutritious. In all the fruits the kernel within the stone contains the bitter cyanogenic glucoside amygdalin, and is poisonous unless thoroughly crushed and roasted (see blackthorn and bird cherry).

Bullaces and damsons

Prunus domestica subsp. institia

The bullace is often spiny and has juicy fruits resembling small, symmetrical plums. They have a strong plum flavour but are not always particularly sweet, although they become sweeter after exposure to frost. They range from purple-black through red and yellow to off-white, and are often mottled with rust-reds. Damsons are generally regarded as cultivated forms of bullace, typically with purple-black fruits, although Lang reports that a cultivated form of bullace with yellow fruits was sold in 1860s London under the name 'White Damson'.

Feral forms of bullace often lack spines and have hairless flower and fruit stalks. The flowers are quite large, with petals measuring 7-12mm long, and the pedicels are downy. The fruits, which grow 15-25mm long, are spherical or oblong and come in a range of colours. They are often somewhat sour, but are rarely particularly astringent. In most bullaces, the flesh adheres to the stone rather than separating cleanly as happens in ripe plums. The bullace's stone is generally quite rounded and swollen-looking, with a rough surface and a blunt edge.

The greengage (*Prunus domestica* subsp. *italica*), is very rarely found outside cultivation, green skin, and has a flesh which adheres to the stone, and a stone which is flat, wide, and has a conspicuously rough surface.

Feral forms of plum are seldom spiny, and have showy flowers and pedicels with at most a few sparse hairs. The fruits are usually sweet and juicy, lop-sided with a marked, one-sided groove, and the flesh separates cleanly from the smooth, flattish stone. The fruits are larger than bullace fruits, ranging from 20-80mm, and also tend to be more obviously lopsided than bullaces.

Top: bullace tree in fruit.
Above: harvested bullace fruits.

211

Cherry plum

Prunus cerasifera

The cherry plum has slightly drooping branches with spiny tips. It is the earliest plum to flower, with the showy flowers opening around mid-March. Like cherries, the fruits hang singly on stalks of up to 15mm, and are rounded and often a rich red colour. However, with a diameter of 20-30mm, they are much larger then any cherry. They are described as 'melting, very juicy, and with 'a pleasant, lively, subacid flavour'. However, we find the texture rather liquid and the flavour quite sweet, although exposure to frost significantly increases their acidity.

Bird cherry

Prunus padus

The bird-cherry tree is generally small to medium-sized. It grows abundantly in moist temperate woodlands. Its concentration in rainier regions suggests that in the Atlantic Period (the late Mesolithic), bird cherry would have been very abundant throughout most of the British Isles, and would probably have fruited prolifically. Today, it dominates the strips of woodland bordering streams and ditch-banks. It also has a tendency to sucker, so often forms dense thickets that can invade pastures.

In its preferred stream-side locations, bird cherry is easily mistaken for one of the broad-leaved willows, especially in autumn when the soft yellow of its leaves becomes suffused with pink. You can tell the difference, though, by the bird cherry's characteristic trusses of small jet-black berries. In May and June, bird-cherry trees are instantly recognisable by their long, drooping racemes of heavily-scented white flowers. We found the flowers rather nitter eating. I tried harvesting bird-cherry fruits from a range of trees in Scotland by beating them in the usual way, but

Bird-cherry leaves turning colour in autumn and, from a distance, superficially resembling a sallow (broad-leaved willow).

212

in every case the fruits were too tenaciously attached to their stalks. More vigorous beating only smashed the fruits on the tree. The only effective way to harvest them, I concluded, is by picking.

In his authoritative and remarkably comprehensive *Complete Book of British Berries*, David Lang (1987: 108) lists bird cherry as "poisonous" and describes the translucent green flesh of the fruits as having an "unpleasant foetid odour and a foul taste which dries the mouth". Personally, though, I find the flavour of the ripe fruits rather pleasant, albeit with a slight astringency, bitterness and an almond aroma, which betrays the presence of the poison that realises hydrogen cyanide (HCN) when the flesh is crushed.

The same toxins are present in the kernel of the fruit-pit, but they can theoretically be detoxified in order to make use of the pit's rich reserves of starch, oil and protein. However, the pits of bird cherry seem to me to be too small for the kernels to be worth extracting individually. The solution was provided by the Nanai, Ulchi, Orok and Udegai peoples of the Amur Valley of the Russian Far East continued to live as hunter-gatherers well into the 1940s. They explained to Anderson (1998), then a doctoral student of UCL Institue of Archaeology, that bird-cherry fruits were one of their most heavily-used wild foods. They pounded the fruits with a wooden pestle and mortar until the stones were thoroughly fragmented and the flesh and kernels crushed. The mixture was then spread on a flat surface, squeezed into thin cakes, and roasted after a period of curing until all trace of the smell of bitter almonds had disappeared. The cakes dried into a gritty fruit leather that could be stored over the winter.

Top: the familiar racemes of small, black fruits laced with
cyanide. Early September, Rothiemurchus.
Middle: harvested bird-cherries.
Above: Gordon bending down branches of a bird-cherry
tree and picking the fruits. (They cannot be harvested by
beating.) Glen Affric, early September.

Intact bird-cherries being crushed with a local river pebble
on a naturally-occurring slab of slate to pulverize the
flesh, pit and kernel as part of a process to eliminate the
cyanide. The photo shows (bottom to top) some intact
fruits, some lightly crushed fruit, crushings with the pits
well pulverized, and a cake ready for toasting. Tools such
as this slab and pebble would not necessarily be recognized
as ancient tools on an archaeological site on rocky terrain,
and this might explain the lack of grinding tools identified
on Mesolithic sites in the British Isles.

Top: newly emerging hawthorn leaves make a tasty wayside nibble.
Above: tree in fruit in primaeval hazel woodland, Western Ross, Scotland, late October.

Top: the edible flowers of hawthorn in mid-May. They're best eaten while they're sill in bud.
Above: Ray harvesting haws. New Forest, early October.

Top: haws cleaned of twigs and leaves.

Above: mush from crushed haws (with most of stones

stalks and skins removed) setting in bowl.

Top: haw mush now set and inverted.

Above: gelatinised mush with the eliminated stones

and skins discarded on the ground.

The widely naturalised Himalayan cotoneaster.

Cotoneasters
Cotoneaster spp.

At least two species of this garden favourite are now well established in the wild and still spreading. The first is the wall cotoneaster (*C. horizontalis*). This prostrate shrub is now found in great profusion on cliffs and downs. In autumn it becomes a mass of berries, which, although rather insipid and dry-fleshed, can be eaten as a perfectly acceptable, if not very inspiring, wayside snack. The Himalayan cotoneaster (*C. simonsii*) is also quite common in copses and waste places, and the berries, although edible, are even less palatable than those of the wall cotoneaster. However, we know of no tests proving their safety, so we recommend that you do not eat them.

Rowan or Mountain Ash

Sorbus aucuparia

The name Rowan derives from the Gaelic rudha-an, 'the red one'. It is also known as the Mountain Ash because its leaves superficially resemble those of the ash tree. Rowan is generally a fairly slender tree and grows up to about 15 or 20 metres, with a smooth silvery-grey bark; however, most trees are much smaller. The tree has traditionally been planted outside dwelling-places to ward off evil, and boughs of it were often hung in barns and animal stalls, for the same purpose.

The creamy white flowers appear in May, before giving way to the clusters of red berries that appear in September. The fruits of the rowan tree are again pomes, so they have an internal structure just like miniature apples.

The fruits as food?

The literature has a range of recommendations for ways of preparing rowan fruits as food. We have tried all that we could find, amounting to 16 different methods involving different combinations of drying, freezing, roasting, steaming, stewing and pickling. All the results were distinctly unpalatable, so we think it most unlikely that rowan berries made a regular and substantial contribution to the human diet in prehistory.

Also, the berries contain a number of toxic compounds. There is evidence that they can cause poisoning, and some of the symptoms – convulsions, respiratory distress – are quite alarming, so beware.

The Apple Tribe

This tribe includes the apple, pear, medlar, quince, service tree, whitebeam, mountain ash, hawthorn and cotoneaster. All of these plants have two things in common; firstly they are woody perennials, and secondly their fruits are 'pomes'. Pomes are fruits made up of complex layers; the seed or seeds in the middle, ovary or carpel wall, one or two of the various layers of the hypanthium.

Wild Service Tree or Chequers
Sorbus torminalis

This tree only becomes conspicuous in the autumn, when its flame-shaped leaves develop a corresponding array of fiery colours, from golden-yellow through all shades of red. The trees are generally fairly slim and grow up to about 13 metres. They have a fairly thin distribution throughout clay and limestone woods in England and Wales and are found mostly in the Midlands and southeast England.

Around May the tree produces flowers that resemble rowan flowers. The small pear-shaped fruits follow in late summer. Young fruits are astringent, but after the first frosts, they turn a brownish colour and become so soft that it is almost impossible to pick them without squishing them. At this stage they are very palatable; you can eat them straight from the tree. However like apple pips, those of the service tree cyanogenic glycosides called amygdalin. But, unlike apple pips. these are soft and we find ourselves automaticlly crunching them up. So, we recommend the fruits and seeds be pounded to a pulp and allowed to 'cure' for a coule of days, then roasted to drive off the last of the hydrogen cyanide.

Top left: soft, brown, bletted fruits of the wild service tree in mid-November - just ready for harvest.
Top right: there are also 6 firm, yellow, unripe ones in the basket.
Middle left: the reddish, cyanide-containing, but dangerously thin-skinned, pips.
Bottom left: fruits and seeds being crushed with stone pestle and mortar.
Bottom right: paste pressed into cakes, left to 'cure' for two days and then baked.

Top: crab-apples.

Above: snacking on fallen crab-apples in hawthorn-crabapple woodland in the Sussex Weald.

Mid-November.

Crab-Apple
Malus sylvestris

An example of the tremendous importance of local knowledge to our ancestors is that there is some variation among wild crab-apple trees. The fruit of some trees seems to resist any attempt to sweeten it, while fruit from other trees sweetens quite readily. It's easy to imagine that our ancestors, moving through the ancient wild forest, would have learned which trees were the best ones to visit.

The crab-apple is quite common and widespread throughout the whole of the British Isles except northernmost Scotland. It is particularly abundant in southern England, and favours south-facing slopes and well-drained soils without too much competition from other trees. The trees can grow to over ten metres tall and usually have a round crown and rough, scaly, or sometimes spiny, bark.

Crab-apples are best gathered after the first frosts, and are best roasted or baked. If you want to keep the fruit for later on in the autumn or winter, then you must ensure that they don't bruise, by plucking rather than beating them from the tree or having something under the tree to cushion their fall.

The vitamin content of crab-apples is relatively poor, but they do have other nutritionally valuable compounds. For example, they contain 1 per cent pectin, which decreases the amount of cholesterol in the blood, as well as malic and citric acids, and minerals including potassium, magnesium, phosphorous, calcium, iron, sulphur and manganese.

Wild Pear

Pyrus pyraster

The wild pear is very different from the domestic pear tree. It can be either a spiny shrub or tree that can grow up to 15 metres tall. The leaves are small and round, with a long stalk. The fruits, too, are small, only growing to about 4cm across, often more or less spherical, and ripening, around October, to a yellowish-brown colour. The fruits are exceptionally hard in texture and virtually tasteless.

We know that Mesolithic peoples in Brittany and parts of continental Europeused wild pears, but we still don't know how they made them suitable for consumption.

The Plymouth pear (*P. cordata*) is a thorny shrub 3 to 4 metres tall and only grows in hedges near Plymouth in Devon. The flowers are much smaller than those of the more common wild pear and the fruit is tiny at only 10 to 18mm across.

Above left: round fruits, as hard as granite.
Above right: the merciless spines of the wild pear.
East Sussex.

Above left: orpine in mid-March with edible shoots and reputedly edible roots. Above right: orpine in flower in late July. Sussex High Weald.

Stonecrop family

Crassulaceae

Orpine

Sedum telephium

Orpine is found in hedgerows and woodland margins, particularly in the Sussex and Kent Weald, although it also has a patchy distribution throughout Britain. It grows to about 40cm high and produces large heads of small, reddish-purple flowers and oblong tubers. The latter can reach up to about 5 or 6cm long by 1-2cm wide.

The tubers are widely reputed to be edible, but we find them very bitter. The leaves are slightly bitter too but do make decent eating and are available almost year-round in the plant's most favoured habitat; fairly wild shingle beaches in the south of England. The small over-wintering shoots are very palatable and make a perfect wayside snack.

Left: close-up of carpet of the **English'** **stonecrop** *(*Sedum anglicum*) in Wales growing over rocks in oak woodland above Llanberis in late May.*
Below: a handful of shoots harvested as a succulent wayside nibble.

Navel-wort
Umbilicus sylvestris

The navel-wort grows out of cracks in rocks and walls and has distinctive circular leaves with stalks going directly the way to their centre, and tall spikes of pendulous pale-yellow flowers in summer. The leaves, which are thick, fleshy and very succulent, are best eaten as a wayside nibble. The tender stalks are edible too, but both these and the leaves bruise and turn into a mush very quickly, so they're not ideal for gathering and taking home.

The navel-wort's distribution in the British Isles is very strongly biased towards the wetter climate of the west.

Top: navel-wort on the coast of County Cork in late December.
Below: the crisp, liquid-filled leaves providing a refreshing wayside nibble. Gwynedd (Wales) in late May.

*Top left: newly-opened
flowers. Sussex, late
March.*

Saxifrage family

Saxifragaceae

Opposite–leaved golden saxifrage

Chrysosplenium oppositifolium

This plant grows throughout the British Isles and favours places that are both damp
and shady, such as stream sides, rocks around waterfalls, and swampy areas in wooded
valley bottoms. It has golden-yellow flowers and its early leaves are very pale and
tender, extremely delicate and succulent. Later on the upper side of the leaves become
dark and develops a scatter of distinctive long, vertically arranged white hairs. The
leaves are round and have rounded the edges, with a very short stalk. The stem of the
plant generally has a covering of little crisp hairs but it is actually tender enough that
you can eat the lot.

This but the base of the plants can be gathered and eaten as a delightfully crisp
salad right through from March until well into October at least. This is undoubtedly
one of our best salad plants.

Top left: dense sward of crisp shoots in July. Banks of woodland stream, Sussex.

Top right: diagnostic features - leaves opposite with scattered, erect, white hairs on upper surfaces, pale undersides, and rounded teeth. Stems are pink with crisped white hairs.

Left: handful of delicious, crisp harvested shoots.

Alternate-leaved golden saxifrage in flower, early March, Harz Mountains, Germany.

Blackcurrant Family

Grossulariaceae

Hand-picking berries and currants is a tiring and inefficient process; beating the bush with a stick yields a much larger quantity of berries, often cleaning a bush completely, and is a lot easier. We use a basket on a long handle, placing it beneath a branch before giving the branch a smart blow with a forked stick. We have also applied this method to a variety of other berries including sloes, and even soft fruits such as blackberries. Surprisingly, only a tiny proportion of the fruits get damaged in this process, and the unripe berries are left behind on the branch to be harvested another day.

Wild Redcurrant

Ribes rubrum

This plant is much more common in our woodlands than is generally realised, perhaps because it tends to grow in out-of-the-way places – often, for example, in shady damp spots beside streams. The redcurrant is distributed widely throughout England, Wales and Scotland, but is not found in Ireland.

The inconspicuous flowers are a greenish-yellow colour and the berries are between 6 and 10mm across.

The leaves are rather smaller than those of the blackcurrant plant, but the easiest way to tell the two apart is that redcurrant leaves are scentless, whereas blackcurrant leaves have scent-producing glands on their undersides and a very distinctive aroma.

Wild redcurrant.

Wild blackcurrant.

Wild Blackcurrant
Ribes nigrum

This plant is immediately recognisable by its leaves, which are larger, darker and shinier than those of the redcurrant, and very aromatic. The berries are black, spherical, between 10 and 12mm across, and taste absolutely delicious. They're also very rich in a range of nutrients; most notably, each berry contains 4% vitamin C, five to ten times more than is found in lemons. Blackcurrants also contain more pro-vitamin A than either lemons or oranges, as well as B-group vitamins, vitamin P (rutin) and a broad spectrum of antioxidant bioflavonoids. They also contain 4% organic acids, which have bactericidal qualities, and 18% saccharides, not to mention potassium, iron, calcium and magnesium. The medicinal properties of the fruit are well known and widely exploited. They're delicious eaten raw, but are also ideal for summer puddings, compotes, juices and jams.

Wild Gooseberry
Ribes uva-crispa

Like the redcurrant, the wild gooseberry is much more abundant in our woodlands than we generally realise; it's just inconspicuous. The leaves are smaller than the redcurrant's leaves and the plant has very sharp spines. The fruits are greenish, and hard even when ripe, and are generally smaller than the cultivated gooseberries we're used to – 10 to 20mm long and between 10 and 12mm across. The surface of the berries is covered with a mass of spiny stiff hairs. Another distinctive feature shared with other fruits of this family is the tuft at the tip of the fruit, formed by the shrivelled remains of the flower. The plant occurs widely throughout Britain, and, unlike other members of this genus, it is as frequent in the north as in the south, except for the far north of Scotland. In Ireland it has a very thin distribution.

Wild gooseberries are best cooked, and make excellent pies, crumbles and jams.

Loosestrife family

Lythraceae

Water purslane

Peplis portula

This is about as inconspicuous a plant as you can get. Usually found creeping along the ground on damp, muddy tracks, it is tiny, with blob-shaped leaves, small, green, practically invisible flowers, and miniscule seed capsules containing minute seeds. Despite this, however, it has long been used as food. To gather the leaves and stalks you should gently lift the mat of vegetation from the damp ground before it starts to form flowers, wash the soil from the roots and eat the lot. The green parts have a very pleasant mild 'green' flavour and are good chopped up in a salad or as a very original side dish. As the plants are so tiny, though, it does take a while to gather enough to make a family salad.

Top left: water purslane growing in a muddy hollow in damp woodland. East Sussex.

Top right: the tiny flowers and developing capsules.

Above: a few of the mild-flavoured harvested shoots.

Purple loosestrife growing by the River Cuckmere in East Sussex. Nuñez and de Castro (1991) report that, in Spain, the tender young leaves are gathered in spring and eaten both raw and cooked. Certainly, they are quite palatable at this stage. However, our experience suggests that they should not be eaten raw later in the year, partly because they become bitter, and more importantly because, in many people, they induce curious (and somewhat disturbing) neurological effects.

Flowering shoot, purple loosestrife.

Elaeagnus family

(Elaeagnaceae)

This is an odd little family, of which there is just one member native to Britain: the Sea Buckthorn. However, it has a number of more familiar relatives, including the Central Asian spiny oleaster (*Elaeagnus angustifolia*), with its silvery leaves. The spiny oleaster is a smallish tree and is planted along the streets of many Mediterranean towns, enveloping them in its sweet, heavy fragrance in spring, yielding sweet, dry-fleshed fruit in summer, and traditionally rated as second to none at deflecting the 'evil eye'. The fruits are occasionally on sale in London and have pits like elongated olives, skin like polythene, and flesh like sugar-flavoured polystyrene, but after six summers living in Turkey in a remote village surrounded by them, I have to admit that I have grown rather fond of them.

Unique features of members of this family include a dense covering of silvery, microscopic scales on the leaves, shoots, flowers and fruits, and, in many members, a profusion of vicious spines. Their wood is also exceptionally hard.

Fruits of the oleaster, south east Tukey.

Sea buckthorn

Hippophäe rhamnoides

This viciously spiny shrub generally grows 1-3m tall. Its roots sucker prolifically, and the bushes often form vast impenetrable thickets on dunes and cliffs around the coasts of Britain. However, habitat loss has greatly reduced its abundance in recent centuries.

The bushes sport silvery-grey foliage, rough black bark, and ranks of short, leafy, spine-tipped side-branches. The male and female flowers grow on separate plants, and throughout autumn and winter the females are covered with livid orange berries. The berries seldom grow bigger than 7-8mm and have succulent flesh, a single shiny brown pip, and a scatter of silvery-brown scales.

The berries smother the branches in their second and third years of growth, and we've regularly counted over 100 berries per 10cm of stem. What's more, they stay on the bushes from late August right through the autumn and winter into early March, longer than any other British berry. For the first month or so the berries are just about firm enough to be picked, ideally with a coarse comb. Thereafter, their flesh becomes progressively more liquid, to the point where they burst the moment they're touched. By this stage the best way of harvesting them is to grip the base of a fruit-covered branch and slide your hand up the stem, crushing the berries from bottom to top and letting the juice drip into a receptacle held immediately below. Most of the spine-tipped side-branches simply bend upwards out of harm's way.

The juice first has to be strained to eliminate bits of stem, dead leaves and other dross. It needs prompt parboiling to preserve as much of the vitamin content as possible. The seeds can be roasted and ground into flour to render them more digestible. The whole berries, pulped, can be shaped into cakes and cooked on hot stones, or turned into fruit leathers and stored for later consumption. In Scandinavia and Finland the berries are eaten as conserves or jelly, traditionally to accompany fish, while in Russia and Ukraine they are made into a sweetened conserve, used as an oil, or drunk diluted as a cordial. But beware: in some people the juice can be strongly purgative, especially if taken on an empty stomach. Charred remains of what looked like a sizeable cache of sea-buckthorn seeds have been identified at the Late Palaeolithic site of Theopetra Cave in Greece.

The berries are simultaneously oily and juicy, and taste very sour, with a slightly bitter aftertaste. They are exceptionally rich in micro-nutrients, particularly early in their season: 100g, or a third of a mug, of mashed fruit gathered at this stage can contain many times the recommended daily allowance (RDA) of vitamins C and E, and concentrations of beta-carotene

equivalent to a remarkable 200 times the RDA of vitamin A. The fruits also contain a broad spectrum of antioxidant flavonoids and oils with fatty acids of both the omega-3 and omega-6 series oils, tannins, malic and tartaric acid, and minerals including potassium, iron, boron and manganese. The seeds also contain oils with high proportions of unsaturated fatty acids.

The various products are greatly valued for their health giving properties in Russia, Central Asia, China and many other countries. The berries are believed to normalise lipid, protein and carbohydrate metabolism, and are also used to treat malignant tumours, gynaecological disorders, gastric disorders, skin diseases, burns and other injuries. They are said to normalise the immune system and counter liver damage in cases of hepatitis. Sea-buckthorn oil also exhibits strong anti-bacterial and anti-viral activit, is powerfully anti-oxidant, and acts as an anti-X-ray agent. It also stabilises blood-sugar levels and is claimed to counter memory deterioration.

Clinical and scientific trials are now beginning to suport a number of these claims. Eidelnant (2003) concludes that "It is difficult to name a sphere of medicine in which sea buckthorn products are useless."

Vast sand-dunes covered with sea buckthorn in fruit, Camber Sands, early January.

Top: female bush of sea buckthorn in fruit.

Above: when the berries are newly formed, they can be gathered almost intact.

Top: another fruiting bush.

Above: the berries crowded onto second-year stems.

Above: sea-buckthorn juice (and discarded skins) harvested by crushing the berries while still on the bush.

Willow-herb family

Onagraceae

Rose-bay willow-herb

Epilobium angustifolium

This is a spectacular plant, with great spikes of rose-mauve flowers with dark purple sepals. It is abundant throughout Britain, on wood margins and clearings within woodland, rocky places, wasteland, and gardens.

The leaves and shoots as food

In the spring, up to about mid-April, you can gather 20 to 30 cm of the plant's new shoots and, later on, the top 20 cm or so of the taller stems. Raw, both the leaves and the stems are palatable, albeit with a slightly bitter aftertaste that is greatly reduced by 10 minutes of boiling or steaming.

The stem-pith as food

Right through to the early autumn the stem-pith makes a perfect wayside nibble. Just split the stems open and scrape out the piths with your thumbnail, a sharp stick or a piece of shell. The pith has a cucumbery taste to it but can also be really quite sweet; indeed it can give a sugar rush that is a valuable pick-me-up.

There is evidence for this plant being used as a caloric staple among the Kamtschadalis in the Russian far east. In James Greaves' 1764 translation of Krasheninnikov's *History of Kamtschatka, and the Kurilski Islands with the Countries Adjacent*, we are given the following account (pp.87-88): "The herb kipri (*Epilobium*) grows in all Europe and Asia has the third place in all the food of the Kamtschadalis. They boil it with their fish and use the leaves as tea: but the greatest use is made of its pith, which, after having split the stalks, they scrape out with shells and, tied up in bundles, dry it in the sun. It is then very pleasant, and in taste resembles dried Persian cucumbers. The Kamtschadalis use it in several dishes, and serve it up green as a dessert. The kipri boiled gives a thick, sweet wort, that makes the best quaffe imaginable: it also affords them very strong vinegar, if to 6 pounds of the kipri they add a pound of the sweet herb of Sphondilium, and fermented in the usual way: they get a great deal more brandy, when they used the infusion of the kipri, instead of water, to prepare the sweet herb for distillation". (In a footnote, he describes quaffe as a not disagreeable Russian drink made of rye malt and flour and very little fermented, sometimes with mint added.) It should be added, by the way, that at this time the subsistence of the Kamtschadalis was based on hunting and gathering as well as on reindeer herding.

The spectacular flowers of rose-bay willow-herb, late July.

Tender young shoots of rose-bay willow-herb gathered in spring and ready to be steamed.

Top: evening primrose rosette
Above: Oenothera sp. *The leaves and root are edible. Hailsham, March.*

Top: evening primrose.
Above: *a single flower. Hailsham, November.*

Inset: Rottingdean village pond.
Above: mare's tail (Hippuris vulgaris).

*Sea holly (*Eryngium maritimum)
growing on sand dunes at
Walberswick, Suffolk. The edible
roots extend for many metres
under the sand.

Cow-parsley on vergeside in mid-May. Cuckoo Trail, Hailsham, East Sussex. BEWARE! Although the young leaves of the first-year rosette are edible, they are often indistinguishable from the unwholesome and commonly toxic rosette leaves of rough chervil and burr chervil, and even the rosette leaves of the deadly fool's parsley. When trampled, the rosette leaves of hemlock can also sometimes look somewhat similar. So ... DO NOT EAT THEM.

Sweet cicely, banks of the Tay, September. The mild aniseed flavour of the leaves make them and excellent addition to stewed fruit and even pancakes; the large green 'reeds' are great in slads and are a tasty wayside nibble. The roots are edible too. Although it is a plant that introduced to Britain (perhaps by the Romans), it has become particularly abundant on waysides in Scotland and northern England.

Carrot and hemlock family

Apiaceae (formerly Umbelliferae)

This family includes many well-known crop plants. They divide into: root crops such as the carrot, parsnip, celeriac and turnip-rooted chervil; plants grown for their leaf stalks, including celery, angelica, and fennel; plants grown exclusively for their leaves parsley, chervil and lovage; crops grown for both their leaves and their aromatic seeds, like caraway, coriander, cumin, dill, fennel and sweet cicely; and anis or aniseed, which is grown just for its seed.

There is a huge range of wild plants in this family too, including great coarse hogweed and cow-parsley. Many of these wild members are edible, but many are highly poisonous, and some seem to oscillate between the two states depending on their environment. For obvious reasons, this last group are particularly dangerous.

The plants of this family can be annual, biennial or perennial, and have leaves that alternate (that is to say, they're not opposite each other) and leaf stalks that often ensheath the stem at their base. The flowers are usually in compound umbels, which means that the flowers sit on little stalks that radiate from a central point, which in turn sit on the large, radiating stalks of a bigger umbel. The flowers are small, with five free petals and five free stamens, and around their base is a nectiverous rose disc, which is often yellow and glistening with nectar. The flowers ripen to a dry fruit consisting of two single-seeded carpels that detach from each other at maturity.

Alexanders (Smyrnium olusatrum).
Alexanders arrived here with the Romans as a pot herb. To this day they are still multiplying, especially near coasts. The flowers are unmistakable, with their yellow petals, shiny green foliage and, later on, large black seeds.

DEADLY POISONOUS! Hemlock with typical glaucous, purple-blotched stems and leaf rosettes that, when trampled look, similar to those of cow-parsley growing on disturbed ground, Dinorben Hillfort, Clwyd, August.

Wild Celery

Apium graveolens

Wild celery grows in coastal marshes and other wet places near the sea all round the coast of Britain, Scotland excepted. However, depending on its environment it can be dangerous. A quote from Pierpoint Johnson (1862) is cause for caution. "The wild celery can hardly be regarded as a useful plant, for, though sometimes employed with other herbs to flavour broths and stews, it is unwholesome especially when growing in wet localities, and has sometimes proved poisonous to those eating it. It becomes quite wholesome when cultivated in dry ground, and the celery of our kitchen gardens is nothing but this plant altered by careful culture in rich dry soil, and blanched by earthing up the leaves as they grow." Since reading this we have felt no great desire to try wild celery, even though we come across it quite often.

It is also closely related to the toxic plant fool's watercress (*Apium nodiflorum*), so our advice is to leave it well alone.

Wild celery growing with the common reed in a deep dyke on Farlington Marshes, Hants. Early July. BEWARE! Pierpoint Johnson (1862) warns that, when growing in water, wild celery can be toxic.

Carrot family

Apiaceae

Pig nut

Conopodium majus

The pig nut (otherwise known as the earth nut) is a herbaceous perennial. It's a delicate, small plant, with finely divided leaves and narrow leaf segments.

Pig nut grows throughout Britain, although it is slightly less dense in the Republic of Ireland and inland from the Wash, and seems to prefer the damper conditions of the west of the British Isles. It is a woodland plant – it is very typically found growing in amongst bluebells – and likes partial shade, which makes it a very early flowerer and fruiter.

The narrow, hollow stem terminates in a small round tuber that can grow to around 3 cm across, and which is edible and available year-round, although the plants leave no above-ground markers when they die off. It uses a self-protection technique; the stem that leads down to the tuber makes a 90-degree turn, so that if you try to pull it out of the ground the stalk comes away in your hand, and when you dig down to find the tuber, it is not where you think it is. The only way to do it is to carefully follow the root down, which is quite a fiddle.

Pig nut is very palatable both raw and cooked. Raw, it tastes very much like a chestnut, with the same crunchy texture and can be steamed or lightly roasted in cooling embers. Nowadays it doesn't grow in sufficient quantities to be used as a caloric staple. In the Mesolithic period, however, it would probably have formed prolific and dense swards and could well have been a major foodstuff.

Pig nut plant in flower, Bramb Grove.

Carrot and Hemlock Family

Apiaceae

Ground-elder

Aegopodium podagraria

Despite the name, this perennial is not related to the elder bush, although its leaves are superficially similar. It grows throughout the British Isles, most commonly in garden hedgerows and woodland margins and at waysides. Its leaves often survive the winter, and have a strong flavour that is nonetheless easy to get used to and quite palatable if you cook them as you would spinach. Ground-elder was brought to Britain by the Romans who grew it as a pot herb.

Rock Samphire

Crithmum maritimum

This succulent and stocky plant grows on cliffs, rocky shores and shingle beaches around much of the coastline of the British Isles, excepting Scotland and Northern Ireland. Its succulent leaf segments and yellowish flowers give it a unique appearance, and its flavour is also unmistakable. The young green leaves are good steamed, especially with fish dishes and make an excellent pickle.

Wild Parsnip

Pastinaca sativa

You can gather this plant's roots as early as mid-August; they're still a bit small, but very tender and juicy. They can be steamed or lightly roasted.

As always with members of this family, it's important to properly identify wild parsnip. The flowers are yellow. The leaves are relatively simple; they're with two ranks of leaflets. The aroma of parsnip is, of course, very distinctive; nothing else quite resembles it.

When the only part of the plant visible is the rosette, it is sometimes impossible to distinguish wild parsnip plants from hogweed. This is potentially dangerous as, while the tap root of parsnip is edible, that of hogweed is mildly toxic (despite young hogweed roots being edible). Hogweed roots have an unpleasant smell that might well alert you to them, and a hot, rather acrid taste.

Two other plants that can be confused with the wild parsnip are the burnet-saxifrage and the greater burnet-saxifrage. Both of these are used mainly as medicine but the fresh young leaves can be chopped up and used in salads and added to soups, and so it's not too dangerous a confusion to make. However, the literature does recommend that they shouldn't be eaten in large quantities as they irritate the kidneys.

Top left: roots gathered from shingle beach in early January.

Bottom: left: a first-year rosette of wild parsnip in mid-summer, East Sussex coast.

Above: wild parsnip.

Dock Family

Polygonaceae

It is important to note that many members of the dock family contain free oxalic acid, which, although it contributes to the plants' appealing sour tangy flavour, is also to some degree toxic. Members of this plant family should therefore not be eaten too frequently or in too large a quantity. It is also helpful to eat sorrels, wherever possible, in combination with dairy products, so as to mitigate these effects.

Alpine Bistort

Persicaria Vivipara

This plant grows in grasslands and on wet rocks high in the mountains of north Wales, the Lake District, the northern Pennines and, above all, in the Highlands of Scotland. It's seldom more than 20 cm tall, with a short stout rhizome. In Scandinavia, where this plant is much more abundant, the roots are eaten both raw and cooked. Growing in the bleak mountains of northern Scotland, where other calorific staples are very thin on the ground, the roots of this plant would clearly be very welcome. In the Mesolithic, however, these bare mountains would have been forested.

Alpine bistort.

Bistort

Persicaria bistorta

This elegant plant, with its orchid-like pink flowering heads on tall stalks and tussocks of large fleshy leaves, is famously a component of dock or Leger-Easter puddings in Yorkshire and other parts of northern England. In fact, around the villages of Hebden Bridge and Mytholmroyd in the Calder Valley of Yorkshire there is a world championship dock-pudding contest every year. Even the mature leaves certainly do make good eating in the form of a pudding or a spinach, although only the youngest and most tender leaves are really worth eating raw.

There are claims that the roots are edible. Pierpoint Johnson (1862) reports: 'Although very bitter and astringent to the taste in the raw state, the root contains an abundance of starch, and, after being steeped in water and subsequently roasted, becomes both edible and nutritious. A considerable quantity of the root of this stalk thus prepared is consumed in Russia and Siberia in times of scarcity as a substitute for bread.'

Maurizio(1927) similarly refers to the 'Wurzelstock' being heavily used in many countries but gives no details of any detoxification.

We have tried every conceivable way of making the rots edible, but with no success. Nevertheless the seedsare edible and the entire flowering head are, however, a good wayside snack.

Top: bistort in flower in meadow sward, May. Michelham Priory.
Inset: the flower.

Above left: part of a large population of redshanks.
Above right: a single plant.

Red shanks and Pale Persicaria

Persicaria maculosa and P. lapathifolium

We've combined these two species as they are very similar. Both produce either pink or whitish heads consisting of a mass of small flowers, and a fairly large seed. In the red shanks the seed is slightly elongated and biconvex, whereas in the pale persicaria the seeds are circular and biconcave. When the seeds ripen, they can be stripped straight into a basket, together with the flowers. The flour produced when they are dried, rubbed, winnowed and ground is a little gritty, but is perfectly acceptable fare.

The mild-tasting leaves can also be eaten as a wayside nibble, chopped up raw in salads, boiled and steamed.

Water-pepper by side channel of River Ouse, East Sussex.

Water-pepper
Persicaria hydropiper

This water's-edge plant has narrow, graceful flowering shoots. It is abundant throughout much of the British Isles, although less common in Scotland. The leaves and young shoots, with their hot flavour, have long been used in dried, ground form as a substitute for real pepper. Although they have a convincing peppery flavour and are very rich in vitamins and other nutrients, research has shown that the same compounds that give them their peppery taste also have toxic properties. It is wise, therefore, to use these green parts carefully and in moderation. The seeds, however, seem to be entirely non-toxic. They are large and numerous, and because the plants grow in such abundance it's possible to gather them in considerable quantities to grind to flour. They make rather dry-textured and uninspiring fare, though.

A species that closely resembles the water-pepper is the so-called tasteless water-pepper (*Persicaria laxiflora*). However, it is quite rare. If you do come across it, the seeds can be used in exactly the same way as those of the normal water-pepper.

Knot Grasses
Polygonum aviculare and related species

This is a scruffy-looking plant, with a mass of stems scrambling over the ground. It occurs throughout the British Isles with the exception of the very northernmost Highlands of Scotland, on wastelands, arable land and coasts. The flowers are inconspicuous little structures buried in the axels of the leaves. Stripping the seeds is the best way to harvest them, although it is quite laborious – my average yield is just over 100g per hour. They can be ground into flour.

The knotgrass may seem to have very little to commend it, but a closely related plant, *polygonum corriegioloides*, has been used as a caloric staple by prehistoric hunter-gatherers. Evidence of its use has been found at the site of Abu Hureyra, on the middle Euphrates in Syria, in caves dating from around 13,000 years ago. Other sites also reveal that people continued to eat the products of the knot grass for two or three millennia after the start of cultivation.

Clearly, then, in the past the seed yield from this unremarkable-looking plant and its relatives were thought of as a resource worth gathering; even something that could be depended on as a caloric staple. Whether the inhabitants of Britain in the Mesolithic period ever used it like this remains uncertain, as so far we simply don't have the archaeological evidence to know either way.

Top: flowering shoot of knotgrass. Sussex, July.
Above: rubbed seeds from the branched sprig.

Black Bindweed
Fallopia convolvulus

With its tangled mass of wiry twining stems, and its tendency to invade and infest arable crops, the black bindweed looks fairly scruffy at first glance. Viewed slightly more closely, though, it is actually rather beautiful.

The dull triangular seeds are the largest of any wild member of this family and can be gathered and made into dampers in the usual way. The result is far more palatable than dampers made from most other members of this family, probably because the seeds are large and slightly thinner-coated and therefore contain proportionally more flesh than do the smaller varieties. Today it is very widespread throughout the British Isles, so assuming that it was equally abundant in the past, it could have made a significant contribution to diet.

The trailing or climbing stems of copse bindweed, *fallopia dumetorum*, closely resemble black bindweed, but its fruit have much longer stalks – roughly 3 to 8 mm, as opposed to the 1 to 3 mm of the black bindweed stalks fruit. The seeds, also, are very shiny. However, copse bindweed is not very common in Britain.

Top left: a flowering shoot of black bindweed.
Left: black bindweed growing through a hedgerow.

Common Sorrel

Rumex acetosa

Sorrel has succulent, arrow-shaped leaves, with a pair of downward-pointing tangs. Both the leaves and the young flowering tops have a deliciously sour flavour.

One of the great merits of sorrel is that it makes itself available to us so early in the year. It's already up and sprouting by March and ready to pick right away. It makes a marvellous addition to salads, or served hot in omelettes or with other cooked greens, and it's a perfect, and simple, stuffing for fresh trout. Sorrel soup is also delicious, not to mention of course the Ray Mears special – sweet sorrel tart.

Sheep's Sorrel

Rumex acetosella

This plant looks like a miniature version of the common sorrel, but its leaves are more obviously arrow-shaped and there is a prominent pair of tangs growing from the base of the leaf blade. It grows on heaths in grassland and arable land, particularly where the soil is acid and well drained. The leaves can be used in exactly the same way as those of the common sorrel. However, it's important to note that neither of these sorrels should be eaten by people who suffer from kidney or bladder stones.

Curled Dock

Rumex crispus

This dock is characterised by its long narrow leaves with their wavy, undulating edges. The curled dock is, in our experience, the only ordinary dock whose leaves are truly palatable and not too unsafe to eat. It does contain free oxalic acid, but not in concentrations that make it an immediate threat. As with the sorrels, though, it's important to eat curled dock in moderation and not too often, and if possible in combination with dairy products.

Meadow red with sorrell, in Sussex High Weald, June.

The seeds

The seeds occur in huge numbers. They are also unbelievably bitter, even though we tried all manner of ways of making them edible. After experimenting with every type of dock we could lay our hands on, we concluded that the best species was probably the water dock, *R. hydrolapathum*, which we harvested while the heads were still green and the seeds still relatively moist and slightly soft. Although it was the best, I have to say it was still not exactly palatable and I wouldn't choose to eat it as a staple food.

Ethnographic evidence supports our findings; most peoples with access to plants of this family preferred to use the seeds of polygonums, persicarias and fallopias, despite dock being so abundantly available and producing such huge quantities of seeds. The archaeological evidence backs this up; there are plenty of examples of polygonums, persicarias and fallopias turning up on archaeological sites in contexts suggesting that they were used as food, but very rarely do we find any dock seeds in this context.

Rumex pulcher or fiddle dock is so called because its leaves resemble a violin. Its leaves make good eating, with, of course, the usual caveats.

Rumex scutatus, or French sorrel, resembles common sorrel but it leaf blades are as wide as they are long. It is good to eat and is widely cultivated in British gardens.

Opposite page: common sorrel.

Above: a coastal form of sheep's sorrel, Cork, An Tuar Mor. Late December.

Nettle Family

Urticaceae

Stinging Nettle

Urtica doica

This is without doubt the prince among green leafy foods. There are all manner of different ways of cooking it – it really is the most versatile plant. And, contrary to what is often suggested in the literature, it can be used year round, providing you use the right bits of the plant and gather it in the right locations. As long as a hard frost hasn't cut it back altogether, you can generally find plants that are protected from the frost in sheltered nooks such as under hedgerows, which will provide probably a few handfuls of small shoots. At other times you should try to always harvest your leaves from areas of shade or partial shade, and where the soil is fairly moist. In such conditions, the leaves are much bigger, more tender and succulent, a bright emerald green, and very mild flavoured. As the leaves are bigger, it's also much quicker to gather a decent quantity. Conversely, when nettles grow in full sunshine, especially on drier ground, they tend to be rather tough and unappetising; the leaves are much smaller, fibrous, purple-tinged and bitter-tasting. You should only gather nettles from these open habitats in spring or early summer; later in the year, you will only be able to use the very tips of the shoots. Whenever you gather your nettle plants, it's also important to collect them before the nettle has flowered.

To gather them, I normally pinch out the top little truss of four or so leaves at the very tip of the shoot. Then, working back down the shoot, I pick off the individual leaf blades, leaving behind the stalks. The leaves grow in pairs and I would normally take two or maybe three pairs, although if the plants are very tender and pale green, with nice succulent leaves, I'll take three, four, even five pairs of leaf blades.

Ray discovered how to cook nettle shoots as a wayside snack by wilting them in the flames of a fire. Just 10–15 seconds, exposure to flames is enough to wilt the stinging hairs which inject formic acid into our skin. The shoots are safe to eat. They're delicious and very filling, if a bit mucilaginous.

Nettles are a very good source of protein, making up anything up to 20 per cent of the dry leaf's weight. They also have 2 per cent fats, as well as 100mg of vitamin C per 100g, and quantities of B vitamins, pro vitamin A, calcium, potassium iron, phosphorous, magnesium and so on.

Nettle soup, made with a mixture of other leaves and bulked out with potatoes, onions and garlic, is very tasty indeed and is a favourite with my grandsons.

The small nettle (*Urtica urens*) is also good to eat, but is less convenient to gather as the leaves are much smaller. It is common on disturbed ground and arable fields, in contrast to the stinging nettle, which is basically a plant of damp or wet woodland.

Although there are reports of people successfully making and eating nettle-seed soup, I have experimented with pure seed rubbed, winnowed and ground to form a white sticky goo, of which even a tiny amount was enough to induce a burning sensation in my mouth, oesophagus and stomach.

Top: stinging nettle. East Sussex, early June.

Middle: plucking the shoot-tip.

Above: having plucked the blades from a further node, now taking those from the node below that.

Top: the tiny seeds - rubbed, winnowed, and ready for parching and grinding.

Middle: plucking the leaf blades from the next node down.

Above: stinging nettle shedding seed in early October, Perthshire.

Cannabis Family

Cannabinaceae

Hops

Humulus supulus

The hop is best known, of course, for its use in beer. However, some parts of the hop are edible. The spring shoots, steamed, are very tasty and similar to asparagus.

The seeds, which we normally gather by beating, are also edible, with a nice oily taste.

It is also claimed that hop roots are edible, but we have tried them and I must say that all the roots we have found so far were fibrous and too bereft of edible tissues to be worth bothering with.

Some readers may be intrigued by the fact that hops are a member of the cannabis family. We can report that the resinous female flowers of hops, harvested and dried, do not produce any pleasantly altered state when smoked, although they are successful in inducing a splitting headache.

Top: tips of young shoots harvested in early May from a hedgerow in Hailsham, East Sussex.
Left: the relatively small seeds of wild hops compared with the substantially bigger seed of its cousin – cannabis.

Elm Family

Ulmaceae

Wych Elm
Ulmus glabra

One day in early April, as we walked over a rise towards the woods at the foot of the Downs, the sun caught a group of trees at the woodland edge. The whole mass of trees glowed golden yellow. My guest, a fellow botanist, stopped and stared. 'Why, those trees are absolutely smothered in yellow blossom,' he said. 'What yellow-blossomed trees flower so prolifically at this time of year?' Well, they weren't flowering at all. They were wych elm trees covered in tens of thousands of winged seeds, with each seed set in a greenish-yellow diaphanous disk 14mm or more across.

Wych elms in spring are a remarkable sight and are the only species of elm to produce large quantities of winged seed on a regular basis. They grow in fairly damp conditions in woods, in hedgerows and beside streams throughout the British Isles. A way to identify them is by their very short leaf stalks, less than 3mm long compared to the 5mm of the English elm's stalks and the 10mm or more of the Cornish elm.

The young tender seeds, collectible from around April to May, have a mild flavour and make very good eating, raw or cooked and added to things like soups. Also, Källman says in his book that in Sweden the seeds are eaten as a porridge, but, having tried boiling the seeds for long periods, I can't seem to turn them into anything resembling porridge.

They seeds have a tendency to keep very poorly, even in a refrigerator, and so really need gathering on a daily basis when you need them.

The young leaves, although a bit rough-textured, are also edible. You should gather them around the end of April or the beginning of May, when they're just emerging from their buds.

Top: a mass of wych elm on a tree.
Above: tender young wych elm,
Folkington, April.

267

In ancient woodland.
Glen Affric, September.

Heather family

Ericaceae

Many of us have walked across hillsides carpeted with heathers, heaths or bilberries, or picked our way across bogs laced with delicate, ground-hugging cranberry bushes. Most of these plants are members of the heather family, and they tend to grow as a thick carpet of low shrublets, cloaking mountainsides and moorlands, lowland heaths and the floors of pine woodlands, turning them pink and mauve in high summer and filling the air with their distinctive fragrance. The carpets commonly form a mosaic in which each patch is dominated by one or two species, which vary according to differences in ground moisture, altitude and rockiness. Almost all members of this family favour acid soils, which range from dry, sandy heathland podsols to sodden peat-bogs. The nectar of heather moorland also yields a variety of fine honeys; that of ling heather is rich and viscous, while bell heather's honey is thinner, darker and very strongly flavoured.

Plants of this family seldom grow much more then knee-high, and generally have small, leathery leaves, which are designed to limit water loss in high winds. The flowers are very small, range from purple to pink or white, and have five petals, generally fused together to form pendulous little bells. Tucked into the bottom of each bell is a round ovary with five minute compartments inside, each containing one or more ovules (embryonic seeds). In the heathers and heaths the ovaries ripen to dry capsules that eventually split open, dusting the soil surface with millions of seeds. In several of the other genera they ripen into succulent berries, studding the late-summer and early-autumn landscape with scarlets, maroons and deep, blue-bloomed purples, just as they did 7,000 years ago, when they provided a key seasonal food for the bands of hunter-gatherers roaming what would eventually become the British Isles.

We now also have a member of the heather family that was unknown to our Mesolithic forebears: the purple-flowered *Rhododendron ponticum* from northern Turkey. It is unfortunately now edging out native plants in areas of ancient woodlands such as those above Killarney in Ireland's County Kerry. The honey produced from this plant is also widely thought to be toxic.

Intriguingly, although all the rhododendrons found in the British Isles today have been introduced from elsewhere, pollen records have revealed that a native species of rhododendron did grow here before the last Ice Age.

Cowberry

Vaccinium vitis-idaea

Cowberry is a low evergreen shrub that grows to a maximum height of 50cm and forms carpets over mountains and moorland, particularly in peat-bog areas. It is mostly found growing amidst bilberry, heather and cross-leaved heath, but in the remnants of Britain's ancient pine forests it often dominates the ground cover. The berries ripen in late summer, although thin scatters can often be found through the winter and sometimes even into March.

When they first ripen, the berries are juicy but taste insipid. However, they acquire an acid flavour after exposure to frost. Benzoic and oxalic acid are present, and this makes them mildly toxic if eaten in quantity, especially raw. To avoid problems the berries should not be eaten to excess.

Despite the need for moderation, cowberries have long been an important food for the peoples of the northern parts of Europe, Asia and America. In many cases they have been gathered in greater quantities than any other fruit, reflecting both their abundance and their usefulness. They're particularly enjoyable added to bannocks, but can also be made into jams and fruit leathers. The juice has also frequently been used to make spirits. The Chippewa people of North America used to incorporate the berries into pemmican; the Woods Cree ate them stewed with fish and other meats; and the Nishga used to add the berries to snow and fish oil, whipped together to make a bush ice-cream. In Europe the cowberry, known by its Swedish name lingonberry, is used to make a refreshing drink, while as a jelly it is popular served with reindeer meat.

The benzoic acid that the berries contain, as well as being a mild toxin, is a naturally occurring food preservative. People have frequently exploited this property by mixing cowberries with more perishable fruits for storage. In northern Europe and Siberia the berries were preserved in cold water over the winter, while the indigenous

Top: cowberries.
Above: comb harvester.

peoples of North America preserve them either as dried 'fruit leathers' or by pickling them in fish oil and animal fat. Cowberry is frequently confused with its cousin, the bearberry. However, cowberry plants have a number of distinguishing features, including evergreen leaves with a smooth, shiny upper surface, hairless leaf edges, glands on the undersides of the leaves visible as yellow or pale-brown specks, and berries with remnants of fleshy sepals at their tips.

Cowberry shoots with flowers.

Bilberry shoots.

Bilberry, or blaeberry

Vaccinium myrtillus

Storing bilberries poses many problems because they are prone to fermentation – if left for any period of time they will develop a yeast film and turn vinegary. However, some berries are very easy to store; cowberries in particular are known to contain natural preservatives. In fact, the traditional Scandinavian way of storing cowberries is simply to place them in a container of water and leave them over the winter.

While the cowberry has a strongly northerly distribution, occurring mainly north of the Grampians, the bilberry or blaeberry extends a lot further to the south; it is found in Wales, the West Country, southeast England and the New Forest, as well as across Ireland. Its distribution is however still strongest in Scotland and northern England. The bilberry bushes produce a great mass of subtle blue-black berries with a grape-like bloom, rather than the eye-catching red of cowberries. Harvesting combs,

Close-up of a bilberry.

which cause minimum damage to the plants while filling up the collector's basket very quickly, have seemingly been used for gathering bilberries throughout human history and are still in use today in Scandanavia, Finland, eastern Europe, Poland, Ukraine and Belarus.

Bilberries are of course delicious to eat straight from the plant, but they have a great range of other uses too; they make an excellent jam and are superb for pie fillings and cheesecake. They largely lack the benzoic acid and oxalic acid that are found in cowberries, so you don't have to worry about eating too many (within reason!). Like the cowberry they're rich in all manner of vitamins and other valuable compounds like anthocyanins, which have been linked to the prevention of cancers and heart disease. They also contain flavanoid antioxidants, B vitamins, pro-vitamin A and a moderate amount of vitamin C, calcium, potassium, iron and phosphorus. They are rich in anti-bacterial compounds and are particularly useful in treating mouth infections.

The Alpine bilberry, or bog whortleberry

This plant is largely restricted to bilberry moors in northwest Scotland, although there are a few to be found in Cumbria. It can be used in the same way as the bilberry, but it doesn't store so well and is probably best eaten straight away. Having said that, it's very heavily used and stored by the Dena'ina in Alaska, often mixed with lard or oil before being stored somewhere cool.

Bearberry (North America: Kinnikinnick)

Arctostaphylos uva-ursi

The bearberry looks remarkably similar to the cowberry. It forms a similar carpet of low bushes and the leaves are the same size and shape and, like cowberry leaves, are leathery and more or less evergreen. The flowers are the same pale pink colour and bell-like shape, and the berries are the same bright red.

Although the distribution is also broadly similar, bearberry is more heavily concentrated in the Scottish Highlands and favours rocky terrain, particularly in heather zones below the summits and in 'summit heath communities'. It is in these habitats where the bearberry is often found overlapping with cowberry. It tends to fruit best on the edges of ledges where it has little competition from other plants.

Distinguishing features

Bearberry leaves have a relatively dull upper surface, with a very obvious network of minor veins running in shallow grooves. The pale undersides have no glands or hairs. The berries are generally a fraction wider than cowberries, and are flattened with an apical dimple so they resemble nothing more than small red doughnuts. There is no trace of sepal scars on the top of the berry; instead it forms a 'superior ovary', with, at most, a vestige of the style, or sometimes a tiny dot to show where the style was attached., The flesh of the bearberry fruit is floury in texture rather than juicy, and is rather insipid. The berries have large, hard wedge-shaped seeds.

The berries as food

Although the bearberry compares so unfavourably with both the cowberry and the bilberry, it has in the past been very heavily used as food, both in Scandinavia and in North America, usually cooked, or sometimes dried for storage.

It would therefore not surprise us to discover that our Palaeolithic hunter-gatherer forebears, living in icy tundra-type areas of north-west Europe, made use of these berries.

The Alpine bearberry (*Arctostaphylos alpinus*) is a close relative of the bearberry and is very similar, albeit with black berries that grow in flat mat-like bushes. It is a rare plant, confined to mountain-tops in northwest Scotland. The berries are watery and rather tasteless.

Crowberry family

Empetraceae

Crowberry

Empetrum nigrum

This plant has a strongly northwestern distribution, with particularly high concentrations in north-west Scotland. The small, often shiny, black berries, although quite juicy, can be a bit insipid. Crowberries ripen in August and remain on the plants through the winter. It is said that they are available fresh or frozen until the early spring and that they can even be gathered from under the snow. They're used widely in Scandinavia and North America, both raw and cooked.

Crowberries apparently keep well in a cool place without any special preparation.

Above: crowberry, September, Abernethy Forest.

Borage Family

Boraginaceae

Several plants of this family, particularly borage and comfrey, were traditionally used for food. Usually it was the leaves that were consumed, although there are occasional examples of people eating the roots.

Many members of this family contain variable quantities of substances called pyrrolizidine alkaloids, which are toxic to the liver – it is prudent to limit consumption of the leaves and even more so of the roots. In Europe the most frequently eaten roots of this plant family are those of comfrey and the alkanet, *pentaglottis sempervirens*.

When the seeds of some plants from this family are crushed and boiled in water, they produce an edible and nutrient-rich oil. Archaeological evidence from the Middle Palaeolithic Doura Cave in central Syria suggests that this practice was applied to a range of boraginaceae seeds by proto-modern humans about 100,000 years ago. The value of these seed oils lies in the fact that they are especially rich in gammalinolenic acid (GLA). Although the human body is capable of producing its own GLA from linolenic acid, we do benefit from supplementation as, particularly as we get older, the body can find it difficult to produce enough. The proto-modern humans of Doura Cave presumably observed that they were healthier when they consumed this oil, and so would have been prepared to make the considerable effort involved in extracting the oil from the seeds. Whether this practise continued among later populations we do not know.

Comfrey

Symphytum officinale

This imposing, heavily-branched herbaceous perennial grows to well over a metre tall, with large, spear-shaped, hairy leaves. The pendulous trusses of flowers range in colour from creamy white through to pink or purple. The roots are large and fleshy.

When harvesting the leaves without the flowering tops present, you need to be very careful to ensure that you are not picking foxglove leaves, as the leafy tussocks two plants can look very similar to each other. For details of the differences, see the photos in the appendix. Foxgloves are deadly poisonous and a mistake like this could literally cost you your life. Young comfrey leaves are good chopped up in salads, and older leaves can be fried in omelettes or pancakes, steamed or used in soups. However, comfrey leaves should not be eaten too often or in too great a quantity because of the toxic alkaloids they contain.

Comfrey roots are often said to be edible, but our advice is not to eat them.

Left: flowers of comfrey, East Sussex.
Above: flowers of alkanet growing as a garden weed, Brighton, late May.

Alkanet

Pentaglottis sempervirens

This plant is increasingly abundant in Britain, and is indeed now considered a weed in the south of England. It looks superficially similar to comfrey, although it's not as tall, has wide-open, vibrantly blue flowers with a white centre, and rich green leaves. Its roots are fleshy, very brittle and pleasantly mid-flavoured, but in view of the possibility that they contain pyrrolizidine alkaloids, I recommend that you do not eat them (tests are currently being organised).

Borage
Borago officinalis

Borage is an annual, and in a matter of weeks it grows from seed to a spectacular superstructure – a mass of branches terminating in the most amazing array of vibrant blue flowers with white centres and purple stamens. The younger leaves are good in omelettes, salads and soups and the flowers can be used as a salad garnish. Once again, however, because of the toxins present in so many members of this plant family, we suggest that borage not be eaten too often or in too great a quantity.

Forget-me-nots
Myosotis spp.

We have tried eating the leaves off one perennial species of this plant and they were excellent, as were all the annual forget-me-nots we tried. However, as with many members of this family, there is a good chance that they contain toxins. For the moment we recommend avoiding them.

Viper's Bugloss
Echium vulgare

This is a typical biennial, which, by mid-August, has normally developed narrow, spearhead-shaped leaves around 25cm long, the youngest of which are edible raw and very pleasant. Although we have tried the root and it was quite palatable, there was a slightly suspicious background flavour, so our advice is to avoid eating them, especially as they might contain liver-toxic alkaloids. The seeds, however, represent the most promising source of edible oils of any of our native borage family, although they have thick coats.

Above left: one of the annual species of forget-me-nots already forming substantial over-wintering tussocks of tender, if slightly bristly, leaves. Perthshire, mid-September.
Above right: the flowers in May.

Top: viper's bugloss - plants growing at the seaward edge of a huge plantation. Crumbles, near Eastbourne, August.

Middle: bugloss seed and spiny calyxes gathered by beating, ready for singeing.

Above: the seed with a loose layer of hay on top.

Top: tender, edible leaves at centre of overwintering rosette. February, Crumbles.

Middle: a thin spread of bugloss calyxes and seed ready for singeing.

Above: burning off the thin cover of hay to singe the seeds.

Top: residue from the burning.

Middle: fine sieving the rubbed residue.

Above: fine winnowing.

Top: rubbing the residue from the burning.

Middle: the fine residue from fine sieving.

Above: the clean roasted nutlets - although some are slightly charred.

Figwort family

Scrophulariaceae

Brooklime

Veronica beccabunga

This plant has blue flowers and green shoots, which are often available in wet places right through the year. The leaves and sometimes the stem are very tender. The flavour is usually mild with only a very slight bitter aftertaste, and they are good eaten raw as a salad plant. Occasionally, the plants with darker green leaves are very bitter, particularly where there is nitrate-rich runoff. The plants should not be eaten raw if you've taken them from water that may possibly have faecal contamination from livestock, as this carries a risk of infection by the liver fluke. However, leaves from plants in such habitats should still be good cooked. Cooking also gets rid of some of the bitterness, although you should steam them very gently – five minutes is normally enough. Whether or not it's enough to kill the infective liver fluke cercaria, though, I don't know. I suspect that longer cooking may be needed in these cases.

It grows in a wide range of habitats, including streams, ponds, marshes and ditches, right across the British Isles.

Above left: brooklime, small-leaved.
Left: brooklime found to the south-east of Fortingall, September.

The Sage Family

Lamiaceae (formerly the Labiatae)

The sage family is characterised by a number of structural features. First, the leaves are in opposite pairs; in other words any one pair is at right angles to the pairs above and below it. The stems are generally strongly angled. The flowers, which are often spectacular, are bilaterally symmetrical.

Hedge Woundwort

Stachys sylvatica

This plant grows in hedgerows, on woodland fringes and in woodland glades. With its symmetrical ranks of hairy, triangular-stalked leaves and its spike of claret-coloured flowers with white markings, it is quite distinct from its cousin the marsh woundwort, which has narrow leaves and pale mauve-pink flowers. In Britain we tend to think of the hedge woundwort principally as a medicinal plant, but in France it has long been an ingredient of soups and cheese dishes. Very young leaves are even used raw, chopped up in salads, although they're a bit hairy.

Hedge woundwort.

283

The Hemp Nettles

Galeopsis spp

As a group, Hemp Nettles are characterised by having nettle-like leaves with prominent veins. The stems are often very bristly and in some species are swollen just below the nodes, and the calyx cup (the cup formed by the fusion of the sepals) carries five very sharp spines.

The large-flowered hemp-nettle (*G. speciosa*) with its flowers of yellow, purple and white is today a serious weed of arable crops, particularly the brassicas, and especially in Scotland. However, I've also seen it growing in some abundance on lake-shores in southern Finland, and it is perhaps in this habitat that it might have thrived during the Mesolithic in what was to become the British Isles. The common hemp-nettles (*G. tetrahit* and *G. bifida*) have smaller flowers that can be either purple, pink, white or yellow. Although these, too, can infest arable, they grow naturally in riverine woodland. Although we today encounter native riverine woodland mainly in nature reserves, in the late Mesolithic it would have dominated much of lowland Britain, and we can assume that the common hemp nettles would have been a conspicuous feature of Mesolithic vegetation.

The seeds of all three of these species are very easy to harvest by beating, particularly as the plants grow often so densely and in such large populations, and the yield per hour of effort is excellent. However, I was once very ill after eating a tiny quantity (less than 0.5ml) of raw seed paste, so it seems that there is something very toxic in the seeds. There are also reports that some people were hospitalised after eating well-roasted quails which had, in turn, eaten seeds of a related species of hemp nettle. If the people of in Mesolithic Britain had a reliable means of rendering the seeds safe to eat, then the seeds could well have served as caloric staples. However, our ongoing experiments have yet to reveal what methods would have worked. For the moment we recommend that nobody tries eating the seeds in any form.

Top: harvesting seeds of large-flowered hemp-nettle, Glen Queich, late September.
Middle: hemp-nettles on the River Medway valley-bottom, August.
Left: a calyx cluster with the seeds visible.

Red Deadnettle

Lamium purpureum

The red deadnettle is very common on cultivated ground, verges and waste places throughout the British Isles, with the exception of the higher Scottish Highlands. The plants are easily distinguished from other pink-mauve deadnettles by the tendency of the leaves and flowers to crowd at the top end of the shoot. Also, the foliage is a grey-green colour. The leaves have long stalks and come to a fairly distinct point at the end of the leaf.

The plant is best gathered fairly early in the spring, certainly by about mid-April. Unlike the white deadnettle there is almost no trace of bitterness in the young leaves, and the flowering tops have a slightly sweet flavour. Both the leaves and the tops are delicious as a major component of a salad.

Two other similar deadnettles are the cut-leaf deadnettle (*L. hybridum*), a small and not very common plant, and the henbit deadnettle (*L. amplexicaule*). Its leaves are rounded, and those immediately below the flowers have no stalks at all. The flowers are purple. This species also occurs on cultivated ground, mainly on light, dry soils, and is found through much of the British Isles, up to the east coast of Scotland, although it is barely present in Ireland. As with all members of this family, it has a square stem.

The cut-leaf and henbit deadnettles are both good to eat, but you need to catch them in very early spring when the flowers are just breaking out of bud.

Above: red deadnettle, May, Folkingham, East Sussex
- the last of this year's harvest of the plant for salads
(also for adding to soups and omelettes).

Above right : a shoot growing in the shade.

Above left: plants growing in full sunlight.

Ground Ivy
Glechoma hederacea

This common perennial is abundant in shady woods, grassland and waste places throughout Britain except for the north of Scotland and parts of Ireland. It is a creeping plant with small, rounded leaves and purple flowers. This plant is widely cited in the literature as being edible, but it is in fact ferociously bitter, especially when it grows in full sunlight, when the leaves develop a purple-red colouration. However, I always put a small amount of it into nettle soups, just to provide a bit of 'bite'

Plantain Family
Plantaginaceae

Plantains have rosettes of leaves with almost parallel veins, and stalks that bear narrow brown heads and contain large numbers of small seeds. In all plantains the leaves are edible and, if properly prepared, so are the seeds. The best way of harvesting the seeds is to run your hand up the heads and break open the capsules as you go, letting the seeds fall into a basket. Plantain leaves are very gentle on the stomach. They also contain alantoin, which is useful for soothing sore skin and is probably what makes the rubbing of plantain leaves on nettle stings so effective.

Broad-leaved Plantain
Plantago major

This is one of the most common plantains, occurring throughout Britain. The leaves are often as wide as they are long and vary hugely in size. On dry turf the leaves and their rosettes are tiny, whereas if they are growing on well-watered terrain, especially in irrigated fields in warm climates, they can be a foot long. Chopped up finely, the tenderest leaves can be eaten in salads. They are also good chopped up in soup.

The seeds are produced in long, narrow, rat-tail heads, much longer than in other plantains. It is essential not to gather them until the capsules start to break open; when they're still pale green they won't ripen sufficiently and can go rotten. Dampers made from the flour are very sustaining and tasty.

Top: huge plants of the broad-leaved plantain growing at the edge of an arable field near Bignor, Hants, in July. Middle: a small section of an immature head showing the small capsules, each of which contains many seeds. Right: seeds being stripped from harvested heads.

Hoary Plantain

P. media

This plant is 10 to 15 centimetres tall, with rounded, short-leaved stalks and the usual parallel veination. The flowering heads have mauve stamens. The leaves are rather hairy and, if other species of plantain were available, then I think most of us would prefer to go for those. In size the seeds are halfway between those of the great plantain and those of the ribwort plantain. Sieroczewski reports that the Yakuti of the Russian Far East 'boiled the seeds of the hoary plantain to make groats'. In the British Isles the distribution of the hoary plantain seems to be restricted almost exclusively to England, where it grows on base rich soils.

Ribwort Plantain

P. lanceolata

This plant has long, very narrow leaves with the same parallel veination as the other plantains. As with the broad-leaved plantain, if the leaves are cut back you tend to get a regrowth of much larger leaves that are more more tender, paler green and milder in flavour. The leaves of this plantain are invariably much more edible than those of the broad-leaved plantain anyhow, but when allowed to grow in this way they are particularly delicious. They are an ideal ingredient chopped up in salads or even in soups, or steamed and turned into a sort of spinach. Generally, it's better to chop up the leaves before you cook them to sever the long stringy veins.

The seeds of the ribwort plantain are borne on quite short little heads on very long stalks. The seeds in this case are much more easily out of the heads because the capsules fall apart much more readily, so you can pluck them in a slightly under-ripe state. Nevertheless they should be very nearly ready to shed otherwise the drying won't work and the seeds won't be released. The seeds are much larger in this species than in the great plantain. They are pretty tough but if carefully parched before grinding they're fine. And again they taste very good.

This plantain occurs absolutely everywhere in Britain, in great abundance.

From left to right: ribwort plantain with heads approaching maturity.

A mass of heads on a wayside near Rye, Kent.

Large succulent leaves re-growing after being cut back. Arlington village, near Kent.

Seeds being stripped from harvested heads.

Seeds being winnowed.

Above: sea plantain on tidal mud-flats of Cuckmere Estuary. Late July.
Below: leaf of sea plantain showing the diagnostic three veins. Ouse Estuary.

Sea Plantain

P. maritima

This plant grows in salt marshes or on short turf near the sea, and sometimes beside mountain streams. It grows all round the coast of Britain and up into the mountains of the Scottish Highlands. It has long, narrow, strap-like leaves, with three parallel veins running close together, and quite a small head on a long stalk. The head is not much taller than the leaves.

It often grows together with the sea arrowgrass, the green parts of the leaf of which is poisonous. However, the sea plantain has flat leaves, whereas the leaves of the sea arrowgrass are cylindrical and semicircular in cross-section. The leaves make good eating although they have a slightly alkaline flavour. The seed of the sea plantain is much more difficult to remove from the heads than that of the other species and is not worth bothering with.

Above left: stunted plants with flat rosettes on exposed rocks. Above right: large, succulent plant, more sheltered. County Cork, late December.

Buck's-horn Plantain

P. coronopus

This plantain again forms rosettes and has heads on stalks but the leaves in this case are either deeply serrated or branched rather like the antlers of a deer, which explains the name. In some forms, however, the leaves are very narrow and smooth-edged. The size and hairiness of the leaves vary, from very hairy indeed in dry, well-lit environments, to glabrous (hairless) when growing near water in partial shade. Leaves from plants growing in shady places tend to be very crunchy, mild and quite delicious.

It grows all round the coast of Britain, as well as inland on East Anglia's sandier soils. The sea arrowgrass, again, sometimes grows mixed in with the plantains and its semi-cylindrical leaves are worryingly similar to those of the narrow-leaved, smooth-edged form. So beware.

Because the seed heads enclose the seeds really tightly, I don't bother trying to gather the seeds of this plantain.

Above left: the winter shoots of cleavers look quite different and are commonly much less stringy. Mid-January, East Sussex.

Above right: tender young spring shoots in mid-April. Lulington, East Sussex.

Bedstraw family

Rubiaceae

Cleavers, or goosegrass
Galium aparine

This is the plant that you probably threw at each other as children, with the intention of getting it to stick to each other's clothing. It is a coarse plant with little barbs running down the edge of its leaves and the corners of its square stem. Perhaps surprisingly, it can be eaten, although you should only use the tender tips. With the very different-looking over-wintering form, a longer length of the shoot-tips can be eaten, as the barbs are only weakly developed, although they can be a bit wiry. Two or three inches of the shoot tip can be used in spring, but as the summer advances, less and less of the tip becomes useable. It's not recommended for eating raw, but it can be eaten steamed on its own, or added to nettle soups. The shoot tips also make a good addition to omelettes.

Elder family

Caprifoliaceae

Elder

Sambucus nigra

Trusses of ripe berries can be collected and taken back to camp, the fruit stripped off and used to a range of foods from drinks to autumn pudding. The fruits can also be stripped and dried in the sun to make what Roma people call 'hedge currants', to bake in fruitcakes. The frothy cream-and-white blossoms can be used in pancakes or fritters.

The green elder stalks taste bitter and have an unpleasant smell, so if you're making fritters you should ensure that you trim off as much of the stalk as possible before you eat them. For the same reason, try to make sure that no stalk material gets into any other elder dishes. A lot of people are allergic or sensitive to some of the components in the raw fruits too, so we strongly advise that you always cook them.

From left to right:
Elder flower being added into a pancake mix.
A closer shot of the mix.
Being mixed into the buckwheat mix.
The finished pancake.

Valerian family

Valerianaceae

Lamb's lettuce, or corn salad
Valerianella

All five British species of Valerianella are edible, but have a very short season. They germinate in spring, form a truss of leaves, flower straight away and as soon as the flowers are over, the whole plant dies back. You need to catch the leaves for harvesting during April or May. The leaves are tender and hairless and are excellent in salads.

Above: lamb's lettuce in partial shade, not flowering by mid-April - still good eating. Garden weed, Hailsham.
Below: plants in flower in mid-April with the basal leaves already sensescing.

Musk thistle in late July. The disk of tissue from inside the base of the head is edible. (Photograph: David Hillman)

Dandelion and Thistle Family

Asteraceae (formerly Compositae)

The thistle and dandelion family is the largest of all the higher plant families worldwide; it has more species than any other. Its most distinguishing feature is the flower heads. Although at first glance the flower heads appear to be single flowers, in fact they are made up of often hundreds of flowers (and in the case of the sunflower thousands), each of which is fully functional as a flower. The individual flowers are miniaturised, packed closely together on flat disks that form the base of the flower heads. The flowers of some members of this family are ingeniously designed to ensure self-pollination if cross-pollination doesn't work.

Despite having so many features in common, the various members of the thistle and dandelion family also have many differences, which allows them to be divided up into tribes, the thistles being one tribe, the dandelions and their many lookalikes making up another, and so on. We won't discuss them here, but altogether there are eleven such tribes represented in Britain.

Pot marigold in early May, Hailsham, East Sussex.

Pot marigold

Calendula officinalis

This plant has long been renowned for its medicinal properties; it got its first mention as a medicinal herb in the twelfth century, by no less a figure than the famous philosopher, herbalist and Christian ecologist Hildegard of Bingen. Originally native to the western Mediterranean, the pot marigold is now fully naturalised and found in a range of locations across Britain, particularly on waste ground.

The leaves should be gathered no later than mid-April. They have a fine soft down on both surfaces and are mild with a slightly bitter aftertaste. They go very well in salads and can also be steamed, but very gently and lightly; they are so delicate that they can very quickly turn into a mush.

The flowers and flower buds are also edible. However, eating the whole mature flower head raw is a rather chewy experience; steamed, they become much more palatable. The detached florets and tender leaves also make excellent additions to soups.

Daisy

Bellis perennis

This resilient little plant is well known for its medicinal properties as an anti-inflammatory, expectorant, and general tonic for the common cold. It may be significant that daisy plants contain 30mg of vitamin C per 100g – almost the same concentration as in lemons.

The leaves have traditionally been used in salads, although I have to say that I personally find them very acrid and better added to food that is going to be cooked, like soups, pancakes and omelettes. Cooking gets rid of the acrid flavour but the rather pleasant sour taste remains.

The flower buds can be pickled in vinegar like capers. They are good, although not particularly substantial.

Above: a dense sward in flower.
Below left: some flowering heads.
Below right: an example of the huge rosettes that grow in the moist, mild climate of County Cork, even in late December.

Spear thistle
Circium vulgare

When gathering the roots our ancestors would have made sure they had located a spear thistle and not a marsh thistle - the latter has much more ornate indentations to the leaf margins and a more complex pattern of spines. If they had inadvertently dig up a marsh thistle, they would have found a miserable set of skinny white roots, which offer little if anything in the way of food. The spear thistle, on the other hand, has a substantial tap root, up to 3cm or so wide at the top, which can grow down about 30 or 40cm.

They would certainly have known that, steamed or roasted, the roots are excellent, with the distinctive flavour common to many members of this family.

The core of the flowering shoot is also edible. It should be cut when the stem is at least 30cm tall, but before the flowering buds have started to form. The worst of the spines can be cut off with a knife and the outer layer stripped, leaving just the crunchy centre. In this raw state it makes an excellent wayside snack. The spear thistle grows very abundantly in fields and on waste ground across Britain.

Although the marsh thistle, (*Circium palustre*) does not have edible roots, the stems can be eaten and enjoyed raw in just the same way as those of the spear thistle.

Our Mesolithic ancestors would almost certainly have used the roots of the spear thistle, although it is illegal to dig it up today - except as part of a scientific investigation, as here, and with the landowner's permission.

Top: flower heads of marsh thistle.

Above left: a young flower-stem.

Above right: stripping the young flower-stem of its spines and outer skin. (Photographs: Ivan Crowe)

*Top left: leaf rosette around the dead stalks of
last year's inflorescence, early April.
Top right: gathered leaves.
Above: an example of the flowers.*

Chicory

Cichorium intybus

Chicory's spectacular sky-blue flowers are borne on the tangled mass of scruffy metre-long stems that form the chicory plant in high summer. These tops die back later in the year, and the following spring the young leafy shoots are produced from the crown of the tap root. You can either take these young, crisp and crunchy shoots, or cover them, blanch them and wait until they get bigger, unless you like the slightly bitter flavour, which I find rather refreshing. Again, the leaves can be made into a handy wayside snack by wilting them over a fire.

The young roots are fairly succulent and would have been eaten by our ancestors either lightly roasted in embers or steamed on top of the fire wrapped in vegetation. Chicory occurs fairly widely across Britain but is most abundant in the south-east.

Nipplewort

Lapsana communis

This annual, which grows up to a height of half a metre or so, is distinguishable from other members of its family by its very distinctive rhomboidal leaves. The young spring leaves are very palatable raw, but they get hairier until, in May, unless they've been growing in partial shade they will be tougher and more bitter, and the hairs will be more bristly. From May onwards, the leaves are better steamed, although any young leafy shoots that you can find continue to be edible for some time. These plants are abundantly available in woodland glades and wood margins, in hedgerows and on waysides, throughout the British Isles.

Below left: nipplewort - top half of a full flowering shoot.
Below right: tender young leaves of new spring growth, early May, Brighton.

Cat's-ear

Hypochaeris radicata

Ethno-botanists working in southern Europe and the Mediterranean area have found that the cat's ear is one of just 17 wild plants that are regularly gathered for food by traditional farming communities in all four countries: Spain, Italy, Greece and France. This strikes many people as surprising, as cat's ear leaves are generally quite hairy – if not bristly – and have a definite bitter taste. But the plants are abundantly available and much more palatable than most of their close relatives, which clearly outweighs their disadvantages as far as these groups are concerned. We certainly quickly got used to eating the leaves. The bitterness, too, is a taste that it is possible to acquire.

Cat's-ear has a rosette of leaves that, in moist conditions, can develop into a large tussock. Usually the flowering shoots are branched, with each branch ending in a flower head that resembles a miniature dandelion. And two criteria for distinguishing cat's-ear from an inedible lookalike, the autumnal hawksbit, are that the leaves and head ooze white latex if you pluck them and, if you pick out the little yellow florets from the flowering heads you'll see, tucked in between them, attached to the disk, small, soft, white attenuated scales 3 or 4mm long.

Cat's-ear grows in grassy places, woodland glades and fringes, and very abundantly on waysides. It is found right across the British Isles.

The leaves make a good salad ingredient. They can also be steamed and are good in soups, cheese dishes, omelettes and pancakes.

There are two other species in this genus, the smooth cat's-ear and the spotted cat's-ear, but both are relatively rare.

Top: single head of cat's-ear in July, Hailsham, East Sussex.
Above: cat's-ear, mid-June, Arlington meadows, East Sussex.

Autumnal hawkbit (INEDIBLE)
Leontodon autumnalis

This plant often closely resembles cat's ear but it is unbelievably bitter and definitely not good to eat raw. Steaming and boiling the leaves simply turns them into a sloppy sludge.

Autumnal hawkbit has largely the same habitat and distribution as cat's ear, occurring in meadows, waysides and woodland glades throughout the British Isles

Rough hawkbit
Leontodon hispidus

This plant's hairy leaves are similar in shape to those of the autumnal hawkbit, although here their edges are less indented. The flower heads are borne singly on the end of an unbranched shoot and are usually between 2.5 and 4cm across. The leaves have a slightly bitter aftertaste, but are quite acceptable as a salad plant. Steaming and boiling gets rid of any bitterness but doesn't seem to reduce the stiffness of the hairs.

The rough hawkbit is very abundant on woodland fringes, waysides, and in grassland. It grows throughout England and Wales and up into southern Scotland, with a patchy distribution in Ireland.

Lesser hawkbit
Leontodon saxatilis

The lesser hawkbit is abundant on dry grasslands, especially in sand dunes and on waysides.
It has the usual rosette of leaves, but unlike the rough hawkbit, this plant's flower stalks are generally hairless. The flowering heads are much smaller too, at just 12-20mm across. The leaves are faintly bitter and, despite being hairy, are edible raw. Steaming reduces the hairiness, and they are good in soups and omelettes too.

Top: flowering heads of rough hawksbit in late June, near Penhurst, East Sussex.
Above: leaves of rough hawksbit dominating the sward. Late June, Penhurst.

Hawkweed Ox-tongue

Picris hieracioides

There are just two species of ox-tongue in Britain. This one has less bristly, occasionally hairless, leaves, which are a dark green colour with purplish veins. When young they can often be eaten raw, and, once more mature, are good steamed, boiled or wilted in flames. The leaves of the hawkweed ox-tongue's aerial shoots are also distinctive as they have no stalks and the base of the leaf clasps the stem. The edges of the stem-leaves undulate like waves. As shown in the photos, the outermost brachioles are narrow and numerous, whereas in the bristly ox-tongue they are very broad and there are fewer of them.

The starch-rich roots are usually less than 10 cm long but are quite thick. Our Mesolithic forebears will have been aware that, eaten raw, they have a slight bitter tang, which disappears when they're cooked either by roasting or steaming, after which they are very palatable. The roots would have been gathered from the early autumn through to the end of April or mid-May, and probably represented a very important food resource. They are relatively easily dug up and our forebears would have been able to dig up a large number in a very short period of time. It grows across much of England and in south Wales, and is often extremely abundant, especially in habitats such as chalk grassland or shingle beaches and, today, motorway verges.

The leaves as food

Although the mature leaves can be very bristly, the younger leaves are fairly smooth. I often eat the youngest ones raw, although they are better and easier to eat if cooked.

The shoots as food

The young shoots are edible lightly steamed, but once they have reached about 25 cm or so they generally become unfit for eating.

Top left: hawkweed ox-tongue with diagnostic undulate margins of the stem leaves. Late August, Ouse Estuary.
Top right: an over-wintering rosette with edible leaves. Downs above Brighton, late April.
Bottom left: the plant in flower.
Bottom right: flowering shoot of bristly ox-tongue showing heads. Late August. Arlington Reservoir, East Sussex.

Above left: flowering shoot of bristly ox-tongue, Brighton. Above right: the distinctive bristly leaves, Arlington Reservoir, late April.

Bristly Ox-tongue

Picris echioides

This introduced species can be distinguished from its cousin by its much more bristly leaves. The brachioles on the outside of the flowering heads are very broad, and clasp the flowering head rather than spreading outwards.

The root is similar to that of the hawkweed ox-tongue and, had it been available in the Mesolithic, it could have been eaten in the same way, although it is noticeably more bitter. The leaves are basically inedible except for the very smallest and tenderest of early spring; these can be eaten steamed, although they are still rather bitter. This is not as attractive a food source by any means but it is becoming much more abundant than the other species.

For now it is concentrated mainly in the south-east of England and the West Country of England, and around the coast of Wales.

Goat's-beard

Tragapogon pratensis

Goats-beard differs from its cousin the dandelion in having grass-like leaves and leafy, knee-high flowering shoots. The plant lives for 2-4 years, and can have either a biennial or a herbaceous-perennial type life cycle.

The flowers close in the late morning, a behaviour that has given goats-beard its alternative name of 'Jack-go-to-bed-at-noon'. As with dandelions, each of its seeds is suspended beneath a long-stalked parachute, but goats-beard seeds are three times bigger and form magnificent feathered spheres or 'goats-beard clocks' up to 12cm across. Today goats-beard is mainly found in meadows and along grassy verges. where it often grows in large numbers. However, our Mesolithic forebears probably knew it as a plant of woodland fringes and glades.

Goats-beard produces narrow tap roots around 20cm long. Our forebears would certainly have been well aware that the roots of biennial plants such as these were edible from late summer through to the next spring, while in perennial forms they were edible throughout the plant's second and sometimes third year of growth. Although biennial plants are often indistinguishable from perennials, they would always have been able to tell if they had successfully caught the roots while they're still juicy and edible because they exude droplets of white latex wherever the small side-roots have broken off. The roots of both forms become woody and inedible as soon as the flowering shoots start to develop. Once flowering is over and the seeds are shed, the whole plant dies.

Finding goats-beard during the winter would have required a forager's focus as its tufts of very narrow winter leaves blend perfectly with the mass of surrounding grasses. At this time of year goats-beard would have been distinguished from the grasses among which it grew by the fact that its leaves lack the leaf sheaths and ligules that are found in almost all grasses.

Also, the winter leaves have attenuated tips shaped like a skiff's prow, tinged a dull brick-red. At the start of spring the leaves become broader and turn a more livid green, making the leafy little tufts much easier to spot.

Our Mesolithic ancestors would have known that the roots are edible raw but are less chewy and much tastier if lightly roasted in embers, or, still better, steamed over the fire wrapped in bundles of sphagnum or wet grass. They have a slightly sweet flavour reminiscent of roasted chestnuts. However, as in many other members of the dandelion family, their carbohydrate is stored mainly as inulin, which makes them somewhat flatulogenic. Traditionally the root was used widely across Europe and Asia and south into north west India, and in 17th-century Britain it was cultivated widely. For our Mesolithic ancestors, the palatability and probable abundance of goats-beard roots means that they were almost certainly a staple energy food.

The flower buds make good eating, but be careful not to collect the older, bud-like heads that have already flowered and are now forming seeds. The young seed-heads are green like the flower-buds, but are much larger, and generally have a tell-tale tuft of pale bristles protruding from the apex. Eating the young parachutes, raw or cooked, offers all the culinary delights of eating a basting brush. The flower-buds can be rather indigestible raw, too. Eaten pickled, steamed or boiled, though, I find them absolutely delicious. The over-wintering and early spring leaves can be eaten raw, or steamed and eaten as a spinach. They are very mild tasting, a little chewy, and rather uninspiring.

From left to right: goats-beard flower and closed seeding head with protruding tuft of bristles. Early June.
A succulent root oozing white latex and with grass-like leaves in early January (dug up as part of a scientific investigation).
Leafy tuft in early March. The leaves are now broader and greener, making it easier to find the plants and their roots.
Early April, and the plant is now forming a flowering shoot, and root is already inedible.
A mixturer of flower-buds (small) and seeding heads (large).
Flower-buds being harvested in early June - ready for steaming.

*Above: leaf of prickly lettuce,
late July. Hailsham, East Sussex.*

Prickly lettuce
Lactuca serriola

This biennial is one of our most common weeds and grows on waysides and waste ground, on walls and in car parks, across much of the south of England. The plants are often quite tall, up to a couple of metres high, and have streamlined-looking leaves with a margin of yellow spines round the edge and even bigger spines growing out of the midrib underneath the leaf.

Plants growing on very dry ground are generally inedible. However, in damper conditions and partial shade, the youngest first-year leaves can be eaten raw, although they are quite bitter and need to be mixed in with a lot of other salad plants. Steam them for five or ten minutes, though, and the bitterness largely disappears.

Overall, as a source of food this plant is not the most useful.

Soft sow-thistle

Sonchus oleraceus

By mid-April this plant has generally formed a very robust-looking superstructure.

The leaves are a dark shiny green on the upper surface and grey-green underneath, and the flowers resemble small dandelions. The solid and spiny-looking leaves are actually soft and tender - cut off the plant's water supply by severing it at its roots and it will wilt away to nothing in a matter of minutes.

The leaves and stems are easily snapped off and harvested, and with their succulent crispness and refreshing hint of bitterness they make a superb salad. You do have to work fast as they quickly wilt - steep them in cool water until you need them. The leaves are also excellent in omelettes, cheese dishes and soups.

You will find the soft sow-thistle growing on waysides, in woodland glades, and on wasteland. It grows in great abundance right across the British Isles. There can be no doubt, given its widespread availability and its palatability, that it was widely used and appreciated by our Mesolithic ancestors.

Above: soft sow-thistle.
East Sussex, late July.

311

Top: classic sow-thistle leaf-shapes. Hurstmonceu, East Sussex, early June.

Above: crisp, tender leaves gathered for immediate consumption in a salad. Mid-June, Hailsham, East Sussex.

Top: winter rosette with a different leaf-shape. Late March, Hailsham, East Sussex.

Above: rosette with leaves resembling those of a hedge mustard, but unusually tender. Early April.

Spiny sow-thistle
Sonchus asper

This plant, too, relies on air and water to give it its seeming robustness, and will wilt away to nothing if its water supply is cut off. Unlike the soft sow-thistle, though, this plant's leaf spines are for real. It may seem surprising, therefore, that so many field guides recommend its use as a salad plant. In fact they refer to the inner leaves of the winter rosettes, which have quite soft spines and are edible even raw. The same is also true of the first leaves of the new shoots, which start to form around March. However, the leaves that form even just two or three weeks later are only of use cooked in soups or omelettes. And within a further two or three weeks the leaves become entirely inedible. Spiny sow-thistle grows abundantly on arable land, wasteland and waysides throughout the British Isles.

Below right: flowering heads in mid-July.
Below left: wintering rosette starting to sprout. Early April, Hailsham, East Sussex.

313

Above left: smooth hawksbeard flowers in late June.
Top right: overwintered rosette in early April.
Above right: massive rosette with flowering shoots in late June, Hailsham.

Smooth hawksbeard
Crepis capillaris

With its soft, tender, hairless leaves, this plant looks like an ideal salad plant. However, they are usually extremely bitter to the point of inedibility. We encounter occasional exceptions among specimens growing in nutrient-poor environments like dry chalk grassland and waste ground, which are sometimes even edible raw. The smooth hawksbeard grows in a wide range of other habitats, particularly on disturbed land, right across the British Isles.

Dandelion

Taraxacum officinale

Dandelions come in a wide range of species with a bewildering array of different leaf shapes. Identifying precise species is a considerable challenge; because dandelions can set seed without fertilisation, they can maintain a plethora of stable lines of very similar-looking plants.

Both the leaves and the roots of dandelions are edible, and although the leaves are really quite bitter, they can make a useful contribution to salads if used in moderation. You can blanch them to get rid of or at least minimise the bitterness, or wilt them for a few seconds by passing them through a fire.

In the past the edible roots may well have served as an essential staple. Certainly we have archaeological evidence for the consumption of roots from the dandelion group from the site of Dolni Vestonice in the Ukraine, which dates from about 18,000 years ago. At this time that part of Ukraine was sub-Arctic and these roots would have been an extremely valuable caloric staple.

The sample we were given by the excavator was entirely dominated by the charred remains of dandelion-type roots. It has generally been assumed that, as mammoth-hunters, the people of this culture were more or less exclusively carnivores, but the presence of plant material that seems to have been cooked suggests that this may not be the complete picture after all.

Dandelion, complete with root.

Above: population with tops died-back and ready for autumn harvest of mature corms.
Below left: close-up of flowers.
Below centre: Gordon harvesting mature corms of water plantain.
Below right: corms and shoot harvested in mid-August. These were much more palatable than fully mature specimens, but still very dry eating.

Water-Plantain Family

Alismataceae

Water-Plantain

Alisma plantago-aquatica

The part of this plant that is widely cited as being edible is the corm, which is generally 3 or 4 cm across and grows about 15 cm under the mud. There is a single corm per plant, and on stickier clay soils its exhumation requires considerable effort; an effort that is difficult to justify. Whether raw, steamed or roasted, the corms have an excessively dry texture and are difficult to swallow. Water-plantains are quite common throughout most of the British Isles barring northern Scotland. They grow invariably in shallow water and are common on muddy sub-strata, beside slow-flowing rivers, ponds, ditches and canals.

Flowering Rush Family

Butomaceae

Flowering Rush
Butomus umbellatus

This impressive-looking plant produces a tall stem, a metre to a metre and a half high, with a truly spectacular umbel of pink flowers, each one of which is 2.5 to 3 cm in diameter. Generally, flowering rushes don't grow in great numbers. The edible part of the plant is the rhizome. It's not very long, usually only about 20 to 30 cm, about 4cm across and a yellowish colour, becoming brownish-black further along its length. We have tried roasting and boiling them but they proved too bitter to eat. However, Sieroczewski reports that the flowering rush was one of the major plant foods of the Yakuti in the Russian Far East in the Sar Republic. Presumably they have discovered some way of making it more palatable.

Top: the flowering rush. East Sussex, June.
Centre: rhizome with attached shoots.
East Sussex, July.
Right: soloman's seal (see over). Part of a rhizome grown in a garden. (Photographs: Gardar Gudmundsson)

Lily Family

Liliaceae

Solomon's Seal
Polygonatum multiflorum
We tried steaming garden-grown rhizomes this plant's roots over a fire and roasting them in the embers. In both cases the result was very starchy, pretty mild-flavoured and very palatable, although there was a slightly bitter aftertaste.

Soloman's seals.

Arum family
Araceae

Cuckoo pint (or Lords-and-Ladies)
Arum maculatum

This plant is a common sight in British woodlands and hedgerows, and occurs throughout England and Wales, particularly across Ireland and southern Scotland. The fascinating and improbable-looking structure of its floral organs is very inviting, but this should be discouraged as all parts of the plant produce a corrosive juice, and handling leaves, roots, flowers or fruits with bare fingers can cause blistering. The glistening red berries, which grow in a spike shape in late summer, are particularly tempting to toddlers and therefore are especially dangerous.

The danger arises from arrow-like microscopic crystals of calcium oxalate called 'raphides' present in all parts of the plant. Large bundles of a hundred or more raphides are found in special cells which, if the adjacent tissues are dissolved, shoot out the incredibly sharp crystals one by one in quick succession. If these penetrate the mucosae of the mouth they cause immense irritation and inflammation, which can result in death from asphyxiation.

The large size and soft, pliable texture of the leaves might seem to commend their use as emergency loo paper. Our advice is simple - don't!

Top: the fruiting head of the POISONOUS berries, early August, Avon Gorge.
Right: plants dug in mid-March - new corms are only just forming and the old ones are withering.

319

Top: closer look at young arum corms forming, while the old ones wither away. Mid-March.

Above: all the detached rhizomes from an early June collection.

Top: early June and the new season's short rhizomes are now almost fully-formed. These were small plants growing on chalk soil.

Above: in processing the rhizomes to render the starchy flesh edible and safe, we followed the system devised by Marcus Harrison and outlined on his website (see p.338). Here the peeled rhizomes are being grated.

Top left: gratings given six one-hour soakings and stirrings, each time in fresh batches of tepid water.

Above: much longer rhizomes from a third population. Late March.

Top right: gratings that had gone through the repeated soakings and been finely sieved, now drying (on the left) and preciptate from water that passed through the fine sieve (on the right).

Yam family

Dioscoridaceae

Black bryony

Tamus communis

This is the only member of the yam family found in Britain (the family is largely tropical). Its leaves are a very distinctive elongated heart shape, with a long tip and arching semi-parallel veins. In late summer and early autumn, the plant's glistening, red, oval-shaped berries hang in strings in hedgerows looking like gorgeous red necklaces.

Black bryony is restricted to England and Wales, where it grows in great abundance. In the Mesolithic period it would have been largely a woodland plant, growing round the edge of glades, scrambling over low shrubs and up into the trees. If the roots had ever been made edible they would have represented a vast resource, as not only are the plants abundant but also the tubers are often very large and starch-rich. Like the cuckoo pint, though, black bryony contains raphides of calcium oxalate - in this case, bigger and nastier than those of the cuckoo pint. They are extremely dangerous, not only to ingest but also just to handle, as they can cause blistering of the skin in many people.

The shoots as food

The very young shoots, when they emerge from the ground in the spring, can be gathered and boiled or steamed for eating. Boiling is preferable as it is more effective in allowing the toxins to be dispersed in the water. However, shoot tips later in the year have more oxalate present than is good to eat and, although I have eaten just the very tips in late spring without ill effect, by mid-summer the equivalent tips produce quite severe tingling of the mouth and throat, so should be actively avoided. So, if you're intent on taking the risk of eating black

Black bryony in September, between Selborne and Blackmore.

bryony shoot tips, consume only the young shoot tips when they first emerge from the ground. There are many references to the edibility of the shots in the literature for central and southern Europe, but some accounts are potentially misleading as the distinction between the shoots in the spring and in the autumn is not usually made clear.

The roots as food

Black bryony's close relative in Australia, *Dioscorea bulbifera* or cheeky yam, is processed and eaten safely by Aboriginal peoples who discovered it. We travelled to Australia and asked our Aboriginal friends in the Arnhem land to show us just how they did it. We were privileged to witness the entire procedure and to eat the end products.

First of all they dug up the tubers, which is no mean feat in itself; it is very difficult to find them in the dry season when the tops are all shrivelled, not to mention to extract them from the hard ground. They then simultaneously roast and steam the tubers by placing them in a bed of embers, covering them with leafy branches and a thick layer of earth, pouring water into the mound and leaving them for about two hours. The tubers are then grated, and leached in running water overnight.

We tried the same process, and experimented with several others, on black bryony in the UK, but the results were inconclusive. Again, the tubers were dug up strictly for scientific evaluation with the landowner's permission. Even when we did manage to render it possibly safe, the starch content dropped dramatically, making it a less viable resource. Although it is possible that in Mesolithic Britain black bryony could have represented a caloric staple, the only records of groups in Eurasia consuming black bryony tubers are generally vague.

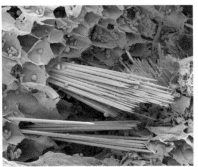
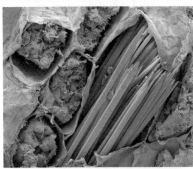

Electron microscope photographs of black bryony tubers: a) cut surface, raw, showing raphides and starch grains. b) roasted tissues. c) roasted and washed for 12 hours. d) washed for 24 hours - no raphides or starch.

323

Common club-rush.

The sedge family
Cyperaceae

Members of this family often look like very coarse grasses. Their stems are commonly triangular in cross-section and large seeds that are either triangular or lenticular (having two convex faces, like a lentil). Varieties like the great fen sedge, sea club rush and spike rush are mostly found in wet lowland areas, and on moorlands you will find cotton grasses, deer grasses, the bog rush and the white beak sedge. The 'roots' and seeds of many sedges are edible. As conditions in the Mesolithic period were damper than today's climate, sedges would have thrived and there would have been an abundance of their seeds available, especially those such as the various club rushes and the great fen-sedge. Indeed, archaeological remains of seeds of the sea club-rush show that they served as calorific staples for the hunter-gatherers of 11,500BC at Abu Hureyra on the Euphrates. However, the seeds of the 75 native sedge species of the genus *Carex* have an extra layer of husk on the outside that has to be removed.

Common club-rush.

Common club-rush

Schoenoplectus lacustris

This plant grows abundantly throughout Britain, particularly in the southern half of England and northwest Ireland, in wet, marshy habitats. It was almost certainly even more abundant during the Mesolithic or Atlantic period, partly because the climate then was much moister and partly because of the loss of its habitat in recent centuries. Its depletion is also partially due to its value as a material for weaving; its soft, green stems are perfect for making products like baskets and mats. Its stems are leafless and grow to around 2 m tall and about 2 cm across.Just below the tip of the stems are small brown flowers that produce the seeds. The plant produces underwater mats of interlocking rhizomes and our Mesolithic ancestors would have found harvesting them was a two-handed job. The simplest way of preparing them for consumption would have been to roast them in embers. However, unlike the rhizomes of bulrush, they have no spongey layer protecting the starch-rich core, so the roasting needs to be done carefully - it is also worth extracting the starch by pounding the rhizomes in a mortar and pestle with a little water. The seeds are also edible, although they are not found in the same quantity as sea club rush seeds and are not such common finds at archaeological sites.

Grey club-rush

Schoenoplectus tabernamontani

This is a largely coastal species, growing in large stands in brackish, marshy conditions, as far as northwestern Scotland. It is distinguishable from the common club-rush by the blue-green colour of its stem and by the scale leaves or 'glumes' of the flowering heads having small brown pimples either side of the midrib.

This species has been eaten by recent hunter-gatherers, particularly in North America; for example the Chipewyan of Northern Saskatchewan, the Woods Cree, the Iroquois, Lake Ontario, the Ojibwe, and the various indigenous peoples of Montana.

The ways of extracting and using the material for food are the same as for the common club rush.

Great Fen Sedge

Cladium Mariscus

This plant's very sparse distribution in the present day is probably misleading. In the last century or so it has declined quite dramatically, primarily because of habitat loss and the effects of run-off from arable land. Under the mild, moist, pre-agriculture conditions of the late Mesolithic period, it would doubtless have been much more abundant and an important food for our Mesolithic ancestors. As well as probably growing in greater profusion in the Mesolithic, tall flowering shoots can produce many seed heads, each containing an enormous number of seeds. Although the seeds are not particularly large, the overall weight of seeds produced per plant can be quite impressive.

Although they have a layer of tissue that makes them dry, they have the advantage that they do not have that extra layer of husk enveloping each grain characteristic of the man species of the genus *Carex*.

Opposite: grey-stemmed club-rush, Farlington Marshes, Hants, September.

Bottom right: harvested short, tender young rhizomes, Pevensey.

Grass Family

Grass seeds are essentially all edible and are highly nutritious, although as yet we have no idea as to the role of grass seeds in Mesolithic Britain. Their main drawback is that the seeds are encased in husks, which are time-consuming to remove. Also, in wet summers, or if the grass comes into flower late (as purple moor-grass invariably does) the seeds are often replaced by the black, deadly sclerotia ('fruiting bodies') of the poisonous ergot fungus.

There are many grasses in Britain that produce edible seeds. The best way to harvest them is by beating them with something like a tennis racket. Yields can be very good – up to around four kilos per hour.

Tufted Hair-grass
Deschampsia cespitosa

This plant grows, as the name implies, in tufts or tussocks, and has dark green leaves with rough edges. When the flowering shoots form, great culms grow up from the tussock about a metre and a quarter high. It grows throughout the British Isles. Given half a chance it can cover huge areas of marshland, and it tends to remain even when the marshland has been drained.

The seeds are tiny, but this actually might make them a more balanced meal because the protein is concentrated in the aleurone layer, which sits just below the surface - the smaller the seed, the higher the ratio of surface area to volume. They also have a higher ratio of protein to carbohydrate.

Tufted hair-grass probably grew in even greater profusion in the damp conditions of the Mesolithic. This, plus its high yield and high concentration of nutrients and relative ease of dehusking, makes us think that our ancestors are likely to have used it as one of their key calorific staples.

Top: a tussock of tufted hair-grass in July.
Ashdown Forest
Above: harvesting the tiny seeds of tufted hair-grass in
early August on Pevensey Marshes.

Tall Fescue

Festuca arundinacea

This is a very tall grass, as the name implies, with a tussock of coarse, wide leaves with serrated edges. It occurs throughout Britain, but is most abundant from the Midlands to the south east. The seeds are very large, the yield per plant is high, and the plants grow close together, forming very dense stands, which makes them easy to harvest.

Although the seeds are fiddly to parch and de-husk properly, they give such a high yield and offer such nutritional richness that we believe our Mesolithic ancestors surely could have used them as a staple.

Top: tall fescue in July. Wilmington, East Sussex.

Above: a close-up of the spikelets

Cocksfoot Grass
Dactylis glomerata

This grass of meadows and waysides is very common throughout Britain. We got a very good yield from the most dense stands, although in more average stands the yield tends to be unimpressive. It is, however, a lot easier to de-husk than the tall fescue, and it makes good eating.

A few heads of cocksfoot grass starting to shed seed.

False Oat Grass

Arrhenatherum elatius

This is another tall grass, with spikelets that look, as the name suggests, like a miniature oat. The grain is rather similar to oat grains too. It grows even more abundantly than cocksfoot. However, because it ripens over a long period of time, the amount that you will actually harvest is much less than you might expect because a lot of it will still be unripe or already have shed its grain. I also find it hard to de-husk. I would put it fairly low on the list of usable grasses.

The literature often makes reference to the bulbs being edible. We've tried them, though and in our view they are quite inedible.

False oat-grass in flower - near Berwick, East Sussex.

Wood Millet

Milium effusum

This plant occurs mainly in England, with a scatter in Scotland, Wales and Ireland. It can form quite extensive populations in shady areas of woodland. It is the only grass that grows to that size in that habitat.

To harvest the grain of this grass we normally just strip it by hand. It matures unevenly, so beating is not an option. It can be eaten as porridge or as dampers and has a very mild flavour; it is also a devil to dehusk.

Head of wood millet.

ACKNOWLEDGEMENTS

A book of this complexity, compiled over a period of ten years, has only come to fruition with the help and support of a large number of people. There are many who deserve our thanks: the list that follows is not definitive and any omissions are entirely the authors' responsibility.

Thanks to our agent Jackie Gill for all her advice and support; Ned Hoste at 2H for making the book look so good, which often meant working well above and beyond the call of duty; Rupert Lancaster, Hugo Wilkinson and the production and editorial team at Hodder; Joanna and Lucy for the transcriptions: Jacqui Lewis and Amber Burlinson for the editing and proof reading. Tim Wilkins at Plantlife (www.plantlife.org.uk) was very helpful in dealing with some last-minute issues.

At the BBC, Ben Southwell and his team did such a great job on the TV series that was inspired by the early work for this book.

A DVD of the BBC television series – with extra material filmed specially for the DVD – is available through the usual retail outlets or direct from www.raymears.com

Photographs

The pictures come from the photographic archives of Ray Mears and Gordon Hillman and were mostly taken specifically for this book and for the planned field guide. Additional photos have been used by kind permission of Tony Brain, David Hillman, Gardar Gudmundsson, Annette Stickler, Ivan Crowe and Willow Lohr.

Gordon Hillman

First, to Ray for his friendship, generosity, and shared exploration of wild foods over the past decade and more, and to Rachel, Ray's dear late wife, for her constant enthusiasm, friendship and support. To my family, particularly my daughter Thlaka, son-in-law Lee and my grandsons Frewen, Kaleb and Eli for their support, sharing in the fieldwork, and readiness to try a constant steam of wild foods, however unappetizing. To Anna Richardson for her boundless enthusiasm, warmth and friendship in working with me in the field, and likewise to Matt (Anna's partner). To the staff of Woodlore, past and present, and to Ben McNutt, Danny Poppet and Adam Crowe.

Also to Dr Tony Leeds of the Dept of Nutrition and Dietetics at Kings College London (KCL) for 23 years of stimulating collaborative investigations of the nutrient status of a range of wild plant foods, and to his expert assistant Rosie Kalukatsia. Also to Professor Peter Houghton of KCL's Pharmacognosy Research Laboratories for invaluable advice over many years and ongoing lab analyses of problematic food plants, and to Dr Tony Brain of KCL's Centre for Ultrastructural

Imaging for his remarkable SEM photos.

Also to Neil Brothers, Arborist Team Leader of Brighton and Hove Council's Elm-Disease Control Unit, and his colleagues, for making us a pair of massive, Turkish-style, elm-wood pestles and mortars to dehusk and then crush tubers of Sea Club-rush, and to Kâmil Bakır of the village of Kızılcahamam for instructing me in the mechanics of mortars for dehusking. To the staff of Woodlore for participating in our experiments with wild foods, particularly Juha Rankinen and Annette Stickler who also kindly made me a superb Pomo Indian style seed-beater. To Tracey Younghusband, Ranger of the Seven Sisters Country Park, for generously arranging access to protected areas of the Cuckmere Estuary and joining us in our investigations with such enthusiasm.

I have also benefited hugely from being joined in field studies by others active in this area particularly Prof David Harris, Dr Sue College, Dr Dominique de Moulins and Dr Andrew Garrard – all of UCL's Institute of Archaeology – and George Willcox of the Institut Préhistoire Orientale at Jalès, Prof Dan Zohary of Department of Genetics, Hebrew University, Jerusalem, and Frances Maclaren of the University of East London, each of whom I worked with on wild food-plants in the Near East and/or Central Asia over the past 20-30 years. Likewise, in Britain, Dr Sarah Mason and Dr Jon Hather (formerly of UCL's Institute of Archaeology), and Tristan Barham and Ian Dunford of the East Sussex Archaeology and Museums Partnership.

I must also acknowledge my debt to the many people from whom I've learned so much in the course of discussions on hunter-gatherer subsistence over the years. In addition to those mentioned above I here include Patricia Wiltshire, Prof Tom Sanders, Dr. Lucy Kubiak-Martens, Dr Mick Monk, Dr Dorian Fuller, Professor Tom Sanders, Dr Peter Rowley-Conwy, Dr Andrew Moore, Dr Theya Molleson, Professor Tony Legge, and Ivan Crowe. Also many former students – now both friends and colleagues, particularly Dr Sarah Mason, Dr Jon Hather, Frances Maclaren, Dr Shane Anderson, Dr Michelle Wollstonecroft, Dr Shona Anderson, Dr John Letts, Dr Dominique de Moulins, Dr Ehud Weiss, Dr Dave Perry, Dr Romana Unger-Hamilton, Prof Glynis Jones, Dr Andy Fairbairn, Gardar Gudmundsson, Dr Ann Butler, Dr Leonor Peña-Chocarro, Dr Mark Nesbitt, Dr Delwyn Samuel, Dr Michelle Cave, Dr Tim Holden and Dr Sue Wales. Again for invaluable discussions and information on ancient diet I am grateful to Dr Nicky Milner of the University of York, Dr Johanna Kufer, formerly of the Centre for Pharmacognosy and Phytotherapy at the University of London's School of Pharmacy, Dr Andrew Ormerod of The Eden Project and Marcus Harrison of the Wild Food School, Lostwithiel, Cornwall.

BIBLIOGRAPHY

Anderson, Shona.2002. *Social History of plant use in among the Taz, Udege and Nanai communities in the Russian Far East.* Doctoral Dissertation in Institute of Archaeology, University College London.

Bean, Lowell John, and Katherine Siva Saubel. 1987. *Temalpakh: Cahuilla Indian knowledge and usage of plants.* Banning (California): Malki Museum Press, Morongo Indian Reservation.

Bieniek, Aldona 2002. Archaeobotanical analysis of some early Neolithic settlements in the Kujawy region, central Poland, with potential plant gathering activities emphasised. *Vegetation History and Archaeobotany* 11: 33-40.

Barrows, D. P. 1900. *Ethnobotany of the Cahuilla Indians.* 1967 re-publication by Malki Museum Press, Banning, California.

Bosch, Hieronymous (1550). *Teutsche Speisekammer.* Strasbourg; pp.35 ff.

Burrows, I. 2005. *Food from the wild: fruit, nuts and seeds, flowers, greens and vegetables, herbs, roots, seaweeds,and fungi.* London: New Holland Publishers.

Cameron, T. 1917. *The wild foods of Great Britain.* London: George Routledge (re-published in 1977 by Priam Press, Dorchester).

Carmichael, Alexander 1900-1971. *Carmina Gadelica* (6 vols in Gaelic and English) Edinburgh.

Carruthers, Wendy J. 2000. The charred hazelnut shell and other plant remains. Pp 407-415 in: Steven Mithen and Nylee Finlay (eds.), *Hunter-gatherer landscape archaeology. The Southern Hebrides Mesolithic Project 1988-98.* Cambridge: McDonald Institute Monographs. .

Clapham, AR, TG Tutin and EF Warburg. 1962. *Flora of the British Isles.* Cambridge University Press.

Colledge, Sue, and James Conolly (eds.), 2007. *The origins and spread of domestic plants in Southwest Asia and Europe.* University College London Institute of Archaeology Publications.
Coultate, T.P. 2002. *Food: the chemistry of its components.* Cambridge: Royal Society of Chemistry.

Coville, Frederick V. 1904. Wokas: A primitive food of the Klamath Indians. *Report to the United States National Museum* for 1902: 725-739.

Darwin, Tess. 1996. *The Scots Herbal: the plant lore of Scotland.* Edinburgh: Mercat.

Eccleston, C. et al. 2002. Effects of an antioxidant-rich juice (Seabuckthorn) on risk factors for coronary heart disease in humans. *J. Nutritional Biochemistry* 13: 346-354.

Ecologistes de l'Euzère (2003). *Les Salads Sauverges: L' Ensalada Champanela.* Dèpot legal 3eme edition: Mars.

Elias, T.S. and P.A. Dykeman. 1990. *Edible wild plants: a North American Guide.* New York: Sterling Publishing. (Reprint, originally published 1982).

Elliot, Doug. 1995. *Wild roots: a forager's guide to the edible and medicinal roots, tubers, corms, and rhizomes of North America.* Rochester, Vermont: Healing Arts Press. [re: cooking of marshmallow roots; arrowhead tuber-gathering; yellow water-lily]

Ertu , Füsün. 2000. An ethnobotanical study in Central Anatolia (Turkey). *Economic Botany* 54: 155-182.

Fern, Ken. *Plants for a future: online-database.*

Garner, R.J. 1946. *The grafter's handbook.* London: Faber & Faber.

Godwin, Harry. 1975. History of the British Flora: a factual basis for phytogeography. Cambridge University Press.

Guest, E. 1933. *Notes on plants and plant products with their colloquial names in Iraq.* Baghdad: Ministry of Agriculture.

Hahn, Eduard. 1911. Wirtschaftliches zu Prähistorie. *Zeitschrift für Ethnologie,* 5:821-840.

Harrison, Marcus. 2005. Cuckoo-pint/lords and ladies - *Arum maculatum.* Website: http://www.countrylovers.co.uk/wfs/arum.htm

Hather, Jon G. 1988. *The morphological and anatomical interpretation and identification of charred vegetative parenchymatous plant remains.* Ph.D Thesis in The Institute of

Archaeology, University College London.

Hather, Jon G. 1993. *An archaeological guide to root and tuber identification. Vol 1: Europe and Southwest Asia*. Oxford: Oxbow Monograph 28.

Hather, Jon G, 2000. Wood charcoal from Staosnaig. Pp 425-426 in: in: Steven Mithen and Nylee Finlay (eds.), *Hunter-gatherer landscape archaeology. The Southern Hebrides Mesolithic Project 1988-98*. Cambridge: McDonald Institute Monographs. .

Hegi, G. 1909-12. *Illustrierte Flora von Mittel-Europa, mit besonderer Berüchsichtigung von Deutschland, Österreich under der Schweiz*. München: Lehmann's Verlag. (10 large vols). (We also used the 1939 edition, where the relevant part of the *Tamus* entry is on p 76.)

Helbaek, Hans. 1969. Comment on *Chenopodium* as a food plant in prehistory. *Berichte der geobotanischen Forschungsinstitut Rubel, Zürich* 31:16-19.

Hillman, G.C.1986. Plant foods in ancient diet: the archaeological role of palaeofaeces in general and Lindow Man's guts in particular. In: *Lindow Man: the body in the bog*, I.M. Stead, J.B. Bourke and D. Brothwell (eds), 99-115 + 198-202. London: British Museum Publications.

Hillman, G.C. 1989. Late Palaeolithic plant foods from Wadi Kubbaniya in Upper Egypt: dietary diversity, infant weaning, and seasonality in a riverine environment. In *Foraging and farming: the evolution of plant exploitation*, D.R.Harris & G.C.Hillman (eds), 207-39. London: Unwin and Hyman.

Hillman, G.C. 2002. Exploring the beginnings of cereal cultivation in western Eurasia. In: A.J. Ammerman and P. Biagi (eds.), *The widening harvest: The Neolithic transition in Europe: Looking back, Looking forward*. Boston: Archaeological Institute of America.

Hillman, G.C., R. Hedges, A.M.T Moore, S.M. Colledge & P. Pettitt. 2001. New evidence of Late Glacial cereal cultivation at Abu Hureyra on the Euphrates. *The Holocene* 11: 383-394.

Hillman, G.C., E. Madeyska, & J.G. Hather 1989. Wild plant foods and diet at Late Palaeolithic adi Kubbaniya (Upper Egypt): evidence from charred remains. In: *The prehistory of Wadi Kubbaniya. Vol 2: Stratigraphy, subsistence and environment*, F. Wendorf, R. Schild

and A. Close (eds.), 162-242. Dallas: Southern Methodist University.

Huntley, Brian and John B Birks. 1983. An atlas of past and present pollen maps for Europe: 0-13000 years ago. Cambridge University Press.

Jørgensen, Grethe. 1974. Unpublished report on archaeobotanical analyses from the Ertebølle site of Ringkloster, Jutland. Journal Number NNU A 5502 at the Danish National Museum. As cited by Robinson and Harild (2002)

Jörg-Thomas Mörsel and Sylvia Thies (eds.) Seabuckthorn – a resource of health, a challenge to modern technology. Proceedings of the 1st Congress of the International Seabuckthorn Association. September 14-18, 2003, Berlin. Humboldt University, Berlin.

Kallio, Heikki & Baoru Yang 2003. Health effects of Seabuckthorn (*Hippophae rhamnoides* L.): Chinese and Russian knowledge and claims supported by Finnish research. Pp. 82-90 n: Mörsel and Thies (cited above).

Källman, S. 1997. *Vilda växter som mat & medicin*. Västerås: ICA Bokvörlag.

Kari, Pricilla Russell. 1987. *Tanaina Plantlore. Dena'ina K'et'una*. Alaska National Park Service.

Koelz, W.N. 1979. Notes on the ethnobotany of Lahul, a Province of the Punjab. *Quarterly Journal of Crude Drug Research* 17: 1-56. [re: edibility of *Impatiens* seeds.]

Krashininnikov, A.N. 1764. *The History of Kamtschatka and the Kurilski Islands with the countries adjacent*. (Translated from Russian by James Grieve). Gloucester: R.Raikes.

Kuhnlein, Hariet V and Nancy J Turner. 1991. *Traditional plant foods of Canadian indigenous peoples: Nutrition, botany and use*. Philadelphia, etc: Gordon and Breach.

Kunkel. G. 1984. *Plants for Human Consumption*. Koeltz Scientific Books.

Krünitz, j.G. 1828. *konomisch-technologische Enzyclopädie: oder allgemeine System u.s.w.* Band 149. Berlin

Kubiak-Martens, Lucyna 1996. Evidence for possible use of plant foods in Palaeolithic and Mesolithic diet from the site of Całowanie in the central part of the Polish Plain. *Vegetation History and Archaeobotany* 5: 33-38.

Kubiak-Martens, Lucyna 1999. The plant food component of the diet at the Late Mesolithic (Ertebølle) settlement at Tybrind Vig, Denmark. *Vegetation History and Archaeobotany* 8: 117-127.

Kubiak-Martens, Lucyna 2002. New evidence for the use of root foods in pre-agraian subsistence recovered from the Late Mesolithic site at Halsskov, Denmark. *Vegetation History and Archaeobotany* 11: 23-31.

Lanska, D. 1992. *The illustrated guide to edible plants.* London: Chancellor Press

Lang, David C. 1987. *The complete book of British berries.* London: Threshold Books.

Lightfoot *Flora Scotica* (1789).

Linné, C. von (1755). *Svenska Flora.* Stockolm

Mason, Sarah LR and Jon G Hather 2000. Parenchymatous plant remains. pp 415-425 in: Steven Mithen and Nylee Finlay (eds.), *Hunter-gatherer landscape archaeology. The Southern Hebrides Mesolithic Project 1988-98.* Cambridge: McDonald Institute Monographs.

Mason, Sarah, and Jon Hather (eds.) 2002. *Hunter-gatherer archaeobotany: Perspectives from the northern Temperate Zone.* London: University College London, Institute of Archaeology.

Mason, Sarah LR, Jon G. Hather and Gordon C. Hillman. 1994. Preliminary investigation of the plant macro-remains from Dolní V stonice II and its implications for the role of foods in Palaeolithic and Mesolithic Europe. *Antiquity* 68: 48-57.

Mason, Sarah, Jon Hather and Gordon Hillman. 2002. The archaeobotany of European hunter-gatherers: Some preliminary Investigations. In: Sarah Mason and Jon Hather (eds.), Hunter-gatherer archaeobotany: Perspectives from the northern Temperate Zone, pp. 188-196. London: University College London, Institute of Archaeology.

Maurizio, A. 1927. *Die Geschichte unserer Pflanzennahrung von den Urzeiten bis zur Gegenwart.* Berlin: Parey.

Mabey, Richard. 2001. *Food for Free.* London: Harper Collins.

Mabey, Richard. 1996. *Flora Brittanica.* London: Sinclaire-Stevenson.

Milliken, William and Sam Bridgewater. 2004. *Flora Celtca: plants and people in Scotland.* Edinburgh: Birlinn.

Monckton, Stephen. 1990. *Huron Palaeoethnobotany.* PhD Thesis; University of Toronto.

Monckton, Stephen G. 1992. *Huron Palaeoethnobotany.* Ontario: Heritage Foundation (Ontario Archaeological Reports No 1).

Moerman, Daniel E. 1998. *Native American Ethnobotany.* Portland, Oregon: Timber Press.

Moore, A.M.T., G.C. Hillman & A.J. Legge. 2000. *Village on the Euphrates: From foraging to farming at Abu Hureyra.* New York: Oxford University Press. (585 pages).

Núñez, D. R. and de Castro, C. O. 1991. *La guia de incafo de las plantas útiles y venenosa Ibérica y Baleares (excluidas medicinales).* INCAFO, S.A., Madrid.

Nyerges, Christopher. 1999 *Guide to wild foods and useful plants.* Chicago Review Press.

Perring, F. H. and S. M. Walters.1962. *Atlas of the British Flora.* London: Thomas Nelson (for the Botanical Society of the British Isles).

Perry, David. 1999. Vegetative tissues from Mesoithic sites in the northern Netherlands. *Current Anthropology* 40: 231-237.

Perry, David. 2002. Preliminary results of an archaeobotanical analysis of Mesolihtic sites in the Veenkolniën, Province of Groningen, the Netherlands. In: Sarah Mason and Jon Hather (eds.), Hunter-gatherer archaeobotany: Perspectives from the northern Temperate Zone, pp. 108-116. London: University College London, Institute of Archaeology.

Pierpoint Johnson, C. 1862. *The useful plants of Great Britain: a treatise upon the principal native vegetables capable of application as food, medicine, or in the arts and manufactures.* London: William Kent.

Pliny. *Historia Naturalis.* English translation by H Rackham: Loeb Classical Library (1950).

Przchewalski, N. von. 1884. *Reisen in Tibet und am oberen Lauf des*

Gelben Flusses in den Jahren 1879 bis 1880. Jenna: Costenoble.

Rackham, Oliver. 2002. *Trees and Woodland in the British Landscape*. London: Phoenix.

Rodwell, J S. 1993. British plant communities. IV: Aquatic communities, swamps, and tall-herb fens. CUP.

Rauber Albert. 1985. Observations on the idioblasts of Dieffenbachia. *Clinical toxicology* 23: 79-90.

Rich, T. C. G. and A. Clive Jermy. 1998. *Plant crib 1998*. London: Botanical Society of the British Isles.

Richter, R.2003. Isolation of potentially oxidative flavanoids of Seabuckthorn. pp.209-213 in: Mörsel and Thies (as cited above).

Robinson, David. 2007. Exploitation of plant resources in the Mesolithic and Neolitic of southern Scandinavia: grom gathering to harvesting. In: Sue Colledge and James Conolly (eds.), *The origins and spread of domestic plants in Southwest Asia and Europe*, pp.359-374. University College London Institute of Archaeology Publications.

Robinson, David Earle and Jan Andreas Harild. 2002. Archaeobotany of an early Ertebølle (Late Mesolithic) site at Halsskov, Zealand, Denmark. In: Sarah Mason and Jon Hather (eds.) 2002. Hunter-gatherer archaeobotany: Perspectives from the northern Temperate Zone, pp.84-95. London: University College London, Institute of Archaeology.

Salmina, Liene. 2004. Factors influencing the distribution of *Cladium mariscus* in Latvia. *Acta Botanica Fennici* 41: 367-371.

Schwantes, Gustav. 1939. *Die Vorgeschichte Schleswig-Holsteins: Stein und Brozezeit*. Neumünster: Karl Wachholz. [Of particular value is the section: 'Schlußbetrachtungen über die mittlere Steinzeit' on pp.144-52.]

Score, David and Steven Mithen. 2000. The experimental roasting of hazelnuts. Pp 507-512 iin: Steven Mithen and Nylee Finlay (eds.), *Hunter-gatherer landscape archaeology. The Southern Hebrides Mesolithic Project 1988-98*. Cambridge: McDonald Institute Monographs.

Sieroczewski, W. 1900. *12 lat wśród Jakutów*. Warsaw. (In Polish)

Spoerke, David G. and Susan C. Smolinske. 1989. *Toxicity of houseplants*. CRC.

Stace, Clive A. 1991. New flora of the British Isles. Cambridge University Press.

Turner, Nancy and Harriet Kuhnlein. 1983. Two important "root" foods of the Northwest Coast Indiians: Sprinrgbank Clover *(Trifolium wormskioldii)* and Pacific silverweed *(Potentilla anserina* ssp. *pacifica)*. *Economic Botany* 36: 411-432..

Tutin, T.G. 1980. *Umbellifers of the British Isles*. London: Botanical Society of the British Isles. (BSBI Handbook No 2).

Vaughan, John G, and Catherine A. Geissler. 1997. *The new Oxford book of food plants*. Oxford University Press.

Varshney., A.C. 2003, Therapeutic evaluation of Seabuckthorn oil in cutaneous burn wound healing in bovine: a clinico-haematological study. pp.104-108 in: Mörsel and Thies (as cited above).

Vebbun, Thomas Jr. 1988. *Wild rice and the Ojibway People*. St.Paul: Minnesota Historical Society Press Watson, WCR 1958. *Handbook of the Rubi of Great Britain and Ireland*.

Yang, Baoru & Heikki Kallio 2002. Composition and physiological effects of Seabuckthorn (Hippophae) lipids. *Trends in Food Science and Technology* 131: 169-167.

Yang, Baoru & Heikki Kallio 2003. Bioactive components of berries of three subspecies of Sea Buckthorn *(Hippophae Rhamnoides* L.). pp 70-74 in: Mörsel and Thies (as cited above).

Zohary, D. and M. Hopf. (2000). *Domestication of plants in the Old World*. Oxford University Press.

Zvellibil, Marik. 1994. Plant use during the Mesolithic and its role in the transition to farming. *Proceedings of the Prehistoric Society* 60: 25-74.

INDEX

First published in Great Britain in 2007 by Hodder & Stoughton

An Hachette Livre UK company

1

Designed by Ned Hoste/2H

By arrangement with the BBC

The BBC logo is a registered trademark of the British Broadcasting Corporation and is used under licence

BBC logo © BBC 1996

A CIP catalogue record for this title is available from the British Library

ISBN 978 0 340 82790 1

Printed and bound by Butler and Tanner, UK.

Hodder & Stoughton policy is to use papers that are natural, renewable and recyclable products and made from wood grown in sustainable forests. The logging and manufacturing processes are expected to conform to the environmental regulations of the country of origin.

Hodder & Stoughton Ltd
338 Euston Road
London NW1 3BH

www.hodder.co.uk